Modern Web Apps using Rust

Second Edition

Build full-stack app on a framework-agnostic core, using Axum, Actix Web, Leptos and PostgreSQL

Nira Talvyn

GitforGits®
ASIAN PUBLISHING HOUSE

Published by: GitforGits

www.gitforgits.com

Printed in India

First Printing: July 2026

ISBN: 978-93-49174-67-2

Cover Design by: Kitten Publishing

Prologue

If I could start with something a little uncomfortable, it would help explain why we're putting out this second edition.

The first edition was pretty much all good. The ideas were kept under wraps. The app ran. But by the time I sat down to revise it, most of the code no longer compiled. The way routes are written has changed since Axum. The GraphQL crate has moved three major versions. The authentication library has been redesigned around the type system. None of those projects did anything wrong. They just kept on going, like healthy software does, and a book that had been accurate when it shipped just stopped being true. That experience shaped every decision in the revision, and it's the first thing I'd show you.

Most of us think that durability is all about picking the right stuff. As long as you pick the right framework, database and runtime, the thing you build will last. I don't think that's right anymore. These frameworks aren't set in stone, and often the ones that everyone's hyped about are the ones that won't last. What you build is what lasts. The limits you set yourself. It's all about the choices you make about what you should know and what you shouldn't. So, this book is a bit different. We built a complete working server, but then we had to rebuild the whole thing on a different framework. It's not about being smart, it's about testing out a new approach. If the architecture is honest, the second version costs almost nothing and the business logic never moves. If it's not honest, it'll make that clear right off the bat. We ran the test, and I let you watch the result rather than describing it.

All the other things we've talked about are based on the same discipline. We don't just go for the latest version of the crate; we pick the one that's been around long enough to trust. We don't tune a connection pool by feel, we calculate it and check the figure against what the database actually permits. We don't say a framework is doing well if the person who wrote it has publicly stepped back. That last one cost me a difficult page, and I'd rather you learn it from me than from a production incident eighteen months from now.

I've found that Rust rewards this way of working more than most languages do, because the compiler is genuinely on your side. It won't let two parts of your application disagree. It turns whole categories of production incidents into build errors, which you fix before lunch. It's sometimes slower on a Tuesday, but a lot faster in December. This book won't make you an expert on rust. But by the time you're done, you'll have a solid head start on building something real, and I'm sure you'll have a much better idea of which decisions are still going to serve you down the road.

Content

Preface

Halfway through this book you build the entire server again, on a different web framework.

This book isn't for practice, but to test out the architecture. All you are learning in this book, is build a full-stack Rust application, on Axum, and then rebuild it again on Actix Web 4, and the domain crate won't change at all. Under both, you'll find a pinned Rust 1.95 and edition 2024 toolchain, business rules that don't rely on any framework, and PostgreSQL accessed through SQLx with queries and transactions that are verified at compile time.

When you're done there, you'll have versioned REST APIs and a GraphQL schema, OAuth2 sign-in with GitHub, JWT claims and Argon2 hashing, and a reactive Leptos storefront compiled to WebAssembly. With WebSockets, you can stream live updates, size Tokio runtimes and connection pools by measurement, then ship to Kubernetes through a gated pipeline. The idea is not to turn you into a Rust expert overnight, but to equip you with the knowledge to build something that will keep on going long after its dependencies are obsolete.

In this book you will learn to:

- Separate business rules into a domain crate depending on no framework, database or runtime.
- Build asynchronous web services on Axum with typed state, extractors and tower middleware.
- Rebuild same server on Actix Web 4 and work with per-worker arbiter model.
- Query PostgreSQL through SQLx using reversible migrations and transactions.
- Publish versioned REST APIs and a GraphQL schema with DataLoader batching.
- Add OAuth2 sign-in with GitHub, JWT claims and Argon2 password hashing.
- Build reactive Leptos front-end compiled to WebAssembly, with server-side rendering.
- Stream live updates over WebSockets, and tune Tokio runtimes and connection pools.
- Containerize with Docker and cargo-chef, and ship to Kubernetes through CI pipeline.

GitforGits

Prerequisites

This book is for anyone who knows Rust and is thinking about web development. It's also for backend or full-stack engineers who are wondering whether Rust is better than Go, Node or Python. You don't need to have any experience with async Rust, Axum, Actix Web or Leptos.

Codes Usage

Are you in need of some helpful code examples to assist you in your programming and documentation? Look no further! Our book offers a wealth of supplemental material, including code examples and exercises.

Not only is this book here to aid you in getting your job done, but you have our permission to use the example code in your programs and documentation. However, please note that if you are reproducing a significant portion of the code, we do require you to contact us for permission.

But don't worry, using several chunks of code from this book in your program or answering a question by citing our book and quoting example code does not require permission. If you do choose to give credit, an attribution typically includes the title, author, publisher, and ISBN. For example, "Modern Web Apps using Rust, Second Edition by Nira Talvyn".

If you are unsure whether your intended use of the code examples falls under fair use or the permissions outlined above, please do not hesitate to reach out to us at support@gitforgits.com.

We are happy to assist and clarify any concerns.

Acknowledgement

I owe a tremendous debt of gratitude to GitforGits, for their unflagging enthusiasm and wise counsel throughout the entire process of writing this book. Their knowledge and careful editing helped make sure the piece was useful for people of all reading levels and comprehension skills. In addition, I'd like to thank everyone involved in the publishing process for their efforts in making this book a reality. Their efforts, from copyediting to advertising, made the project what it is today.

Finally, I'd like to express my gratitude to everyone who has shown me unconditional love and encouragement throughout my life. Their support was crucial to the completion of this book. I appreciate your help with this endeavour and your continued interest in my career.

CHAPTER 1

SETTING UP RUST 2024, ZED AND LEPTOS

Introduction

The very first thing to begin with this book, is to prepare the workstation that carries us through every chapter that follows, and our work stays firmly practical from the very first command onward. Across the coming sections, we are going to install a pinned Rust toolchain, adopt Zed as our editor, scaffold a real Leptos workspace, bring up the data services our application depends upon, and finish with a live page served from our own machine.

The sample application carries the name LibroCommerce, and it grows across the book into a book-selling platform where visitors browse a catalogue, inspect individual titles, manage a cart, and place their orders. We are going to build that application progressively, so the workspace we generate today becomes the workspace we extend in Chapter 2, harden later, and finally ship at the end. None of what we write here gets discarded later, and each file we touch earns its place across the chapters that follow.

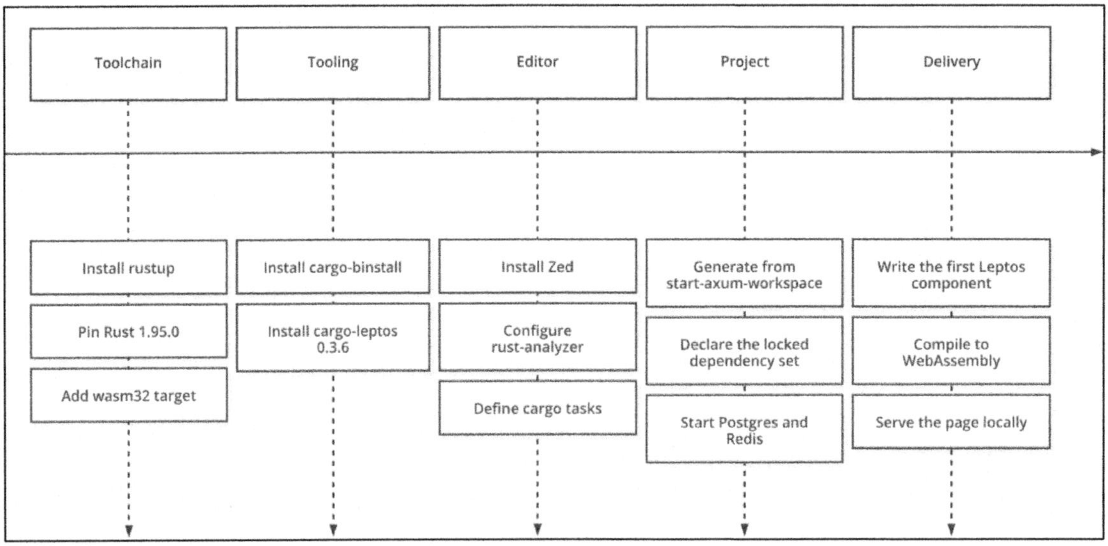

Why Rust for Modern Web Apps?

Rust in Production Web Development

We are drawn to Rust for web work because the language removes an entire category of runtime failure before our code ever reaches a server. The memory safety we gain arrives without a garbage collector, so our request handlers hold predictable latency under load rather than pausing at inconvenient moments. Those concurrency errors that would surface as intermittent production incidents in other languages become compile errors instead, and we then fix them while the cost of fixing them remains low. That trade sits at the centre of every decision throughout this book.

The performance argument forms the second half of the case. A Rust web service compiled in release mode runs close to the metal, holds a small memory footprint, and starts in milliseconds, all of which matter enormously once we containerize our work later and pay for every megabyte and every cold start. We also gain a single language across the whole stack, because the same structs that model an order on the server compile to WebAssembly and render that order in the browser.

The surrounding ecosystem has matured considerably since the first edition appeared. Axum reached 0.8 and settled into a stable routing and extractor design. On the 4.x line, Actix Web has passed its thirteenth minor release and remains one of the most widely deployed Rust web frameworks in production. The SQLx crate offers compile-time verified queries against a live schema, and the async runtimes, HTTP clients, serialization layers, and tracing crates all sit on well-maintained foundations that thousands of services depend upon daily. We are no longer assembling anything experimental.

What Edition 2024 Changes?

We should now separate two ideas that often get confused, because the distinction shapes how we pin our environment. A Rust *version* names the compiler we install, and those versions ship every six weeks with strict backward compatibility. An edition, by contrast, names a per-crate dialect of the language, declared once in Cargo.toml, and editions exist so that the language can make breaking changes without splitting the ecosystem. A crate written against one edition links against a crate written against another without friction, so our choice of edition never constrains which dependencies we may use.

The 2024 edition became usable with the release of Rust 1.85, and every compiler released since then supports it as well. Our chosen compiler, 1.95.0, therefore sits comfortably inside that range. The edition tightens several rules that previously allowed subtle mistakes, and the changes worth carrying forward include stricter temporary lifetimes in tail expressions and **`if let`** bindings, **`unsafe`** now being required on attributes such as **`#[unsafe(no_mangle)]`**, **`std::env::set_var`** becoming an unsafe function, and **`impl Trait`** return types capturing all in-scope lifetimes by default.

A further benefit of the 2024 edition bears directly on the reliability of everything we build. The declaration **`edition = "2024"`** activates Cargo's third-generation dependency resolver, which respects the rust-version field we set in our workspace. When a dependency later publishes a patch that demands a newer compiler than ours, Cargo will select an older compatible release instead of failing outright. That single behaviour keeps our project building months from now, and we shall configure it deliberately in the section on the locked dependency set.

Introducing LibroCommerce

That same application gives every chapter a concrete target, and we will describe its shape now so that the folders we generate shortly carry obvious meaning. The application serves a catalogue of books, exposes detail views for individual titles, tracks a shopping cart per visitor, accepts orders, and pushes live stock and order-status updates to the browser. Underneath those features sit three service areas that we treat as separate concerns from the very beginning, namely inventory, orders, and user accounts.

We are going to build LibroCommerce as a Cargo workspace rather than as a single crate, and that decision pays off repeatedly. These shared models live in one place and compile into both the server binary and the WebAssembly bundle. The Axum backend and the Actix Web backend we add later both consume those same models, so a change to the Order type propagates everywhere at once and the compiler tells us exactly what broke. Every member of the workspace also shares a single Cargo.lock, and that shared lockfile underpins the reproducibility we care about throughout this book.

Installing Toolchain

Installing rustup and Pinning Rust 1.95

We will treat Linux as our working environment throughout this book, and every command that follows assumes a Linux shell. Installing rustup comes first, since that tool handles compiler installation, updates, target management, and component installation from a single interface. A single bootstrap script fetches it for us, and that script needs no privileges beyond our own user account, since everything lands inside our home directory rather than in system paths.

In the script below, we will now download and run the **rustup** installer.

```
curl --proto '=https' --tlsv1.2 -sSf https://sh.rustup.rs | sh
```

The installer offers a choice of profiles, and we shall accept the default by pressing **1**, which brings in the compiler, Cargo, and the standard documentation. At this point the shell still lacks the Cargo binaries on its path once the script completes, because the installer cannot modify a session that is already running. We therefore load the environment file that **rustup** has just written, and every new shell we open afterwards picks those paths up automatically.

```
source "$HOME/.cargo/env"
```

We can now confirm that the toolchain responds before going any further.

```
rustc --version

cargo --version
```

The shell reports the active compiler alongside the matching Cargo build, and both lines should name the same version number.

```
rustc 1.95.0
cargo 1.95.0
```

The version reported may well differ at this point, because rustup installs whichever release happens to be current on the day we run it. That variability is exactly what we want to eliminate, since a book whose instructions depend on the calendar serves nobody well and produces failures that nobody can reproduce.

Understanding 'rust-toolchain.toml'

We pin our compiler rather than tracking the latest stable release, and the reasoning deserves a moment of attention. A book that says "install the newest Rust" ages badly, because a compiler released next quarter may warn about patterns we wrote today or resolve dependencies differently. One that pins an exact version instead behaves identically for everyone who follows it. We have selected 1.95.0, which reached stable in April 2026 and has since had two further release cycles pass over it without ever requiring a patch release of its own.

The Rust toolchain supports pinning through a file that **rustup** reads automatically, and we will place that file at the root of our project once the project exists. Our scaffolding section creates it shortly, though understanding its contents now saves us from treating it as unexplained boilerplate later. The file names a channel, requests the components we rely on, and declares the compilation targets our build needs, all of which rustup then provisions on our behalf without any further instruction from us.

So here, we will then define the toolchain pin as below.

```
[toolchain]
channel = "1.95.0"
components = ["rustfmt", "clippy", "rust-analyzer"]
targets = ["wasm32-unknown-unknown"]
```

Once **rust-toolchain.toml** sits in our project root, any invocation of **cargo** or **rustc** from inside that directory switches to 1.95.0 automatically, and **rustup** downloads that toolchain on first use without being asked. Whoever clones LibroCommerce next receives the same compiler, the same formatter, the same linter, and the same WebAssembly target. That single file removes the most common source of build failures reported between different machines, and it costs us only five lines of configuration.

Adding WebAssembly Target

That frontend compiles to WebAssembly rather than to native code, so the compiler needs a target definition for the browser. The **targets** entry we placed in **rust-toolchain.toml** handles that installation on our behalf, and we rarely need to intervene at all. Its manual equivalent still deserves our attention, because error messages occasionally reference the target by name and we want to recognize it immediately whenever that happens rather than searching for what the unfamiliar string means.

We can now add the browser target explicitly.

```
rustup target add wasm32-unknown-unknown
```

We then confirm the outcome by asking rustup which targets it currently holds for our toolchain.

```
rustup target list --installed
```

The response lists our native target alongside the browser target we just requested.

```
wasm32-unknown-unknown
x86_64-unknown-linux-gnu
```

The name **`wasm32-unknown-unknown`** describes a 32-bit WebAssembly architecture with no assumed vendor and no assumed operating system, which accurately reflects the constraints of a browser sandbox. That server code continues to compile for the native Linux target, while the frontend crate compiles for this one instead, and our front-end work sits almost entirely inside that boundary. Both targets build from the same source tree, and the build tool we install next coordinates those two compilations so that we never invoke them separately.

Installing 'cargo-leptos' and Developer Tooling

A Leptos project builds through a dedicated Cargo subcommand that coordinates two compilations at once, namely the server binary and the WebAssembly bundle, along with stylesheet processing and asset copying. Built from source, that tool takes several minutes on most machines, so we will first install cargo-binstall, which fetches prebuilt binaries whenever a project publishes them and falls back to a source build only when no suitable binary exists for our platform, which saves us a considerable wait.

In the script below, we will now install the binary installer.

```
cargo install cargo-binstall
```

Once this is in place, we shall then install the Leptos build tool at the exact version this book targets.

```
cargo binstall cargo-leptos@0.3.6
```

We can now verify the installation before moving on, since a missing or mismatched build tool produces confusing errors much later in the process.

```
cargo leptos --version
```

The response names the tool alongside its version.

```
cargo-leptos 0.3.6
```

A further pair of tools will serve us well from this point forward, and both install quickly through the same mechanism. We are going to add cargo-nextest for the faster test runner our release pipeline depends upon, and sqlx-cli for the migrations and offline query preparation we introduce later.

```
cargo binstall cargo-nextest sqlx-cli
```

Both installations now mean neither of those chapters must pause for environment setup later, and our tooling stays consistent with the pinned toolchain we established a moment ago.

Setting up Zed

Installing Zed

We have chosen Zed as the editor for this edition, and the choice rests on rather more than novelty. The editor is written in Rust, renders through the GPU, and reached its 1.0 release in April 2026 after a long stabilization period on Linux. Support for the language server arrives built in rather than through separately installed extensions, so rust-analyzer starts working the moment we open a Cargo project and needs no configuration before it becomes useful to us.

The editing loop stays responsive on a workspace that holds several crates, and responsiveness matters enormously when we recompile as frequently as this book asks us to. None of the chapters ahead depends on Zed specifically, and every command we run is a plain Cargo invocation, so those of us with an established setup lose nothing by staying with it.

So here, we will then install Zed through the official script.

```
curl -f https://zed.dev/install.sh | sh
```

The installer places the binary under our home directory and adds a launcher entry for the desktop environment, so no system directories are touched at any point. We can now start the editor from our shell to confirm that the installation succeeded, and any 1.x release serves us equally well for the work ahead, since none of our configuration depends on features introduced after the 1.0 milestone.

```
zed --version
```

The launcher entry also lets us open the editor from our desktop environment whenever we prefer that route.

Configuring 'rust-analyzer' and Formatting

The editor reads user-level configuration from a single JSON file, and we will now edit that file to establish the behaviour we want from Rust projects. This configuration path sits under the XDG configuration directory, and Zed creates the file automatically on first launch, so we simply open it for editing rather than creating it ourselves. Every setting we place there applies across all our projects, while project-specific overrides live inside the repository itself. Both layers merge at startup.

```
zed ~/.config/zed/settings.json
```

In the script below, we will then replace the contents with a configuration that formats on save, runs Clippy as we type rather than plain **`cargo check`**, and enables the inlay hints that make unfamiliar Rust code considerably easier to follow.

```
{
  "format_on_save": "on",
  "languages": {
    "Rust": {
      "tab_size": 4,
      "formatter": "language_server"
    }
  },
  "lsp": {
    "rust-analyzer": {
      "initialization_options": {
        "check": {
          "command": "clippy"
        },
        "inlayHints": {
          "typeHints": { "enable": true },
          "parameterHints": { "enable": true },
          "closureReturnTypeHints": { "enable": "always" }
```

```
          },
          "cargo": {
            "allFeatures": true
          }
        }
      }
    }
  }
```

There are two entries in the above configuration that deserve particular attention:

1. A check.command set to clippy means our editor surfaces lint warnings continuously instead of only when we remember to run the linter, and our release pipeline later turns those same lints into a hard gate.
2. The cargo.allFeatures entry matters specifically for LibroCommerce, because we will place our two backends behind feature flags later and we want the editor to analyse both of them rather than silently ignoring one of the two.

Running Tasks from Editor

The editor lets a project define its own tasks, and we are going to take advantage of that so the commands we run most often stay one keystroke away. Those definitions live in a file we commit alongside the code, so everyone working on LibroCommerce inherits the same shortcuts without configuring anything themselves. We will create the file inside our project directory once the project exists, and it lives under a **`.zed`** folder at the repository root.

So here, we will then define the three tasks we use most.

```
[
  {
    "label": "leptos watch",
    "command": "cargo",
    "args": ["leptos", "watch"],
    "use_new_terminal": false
  },
  {
    "label": "clippy",
    "command": "cargo",
```

```
    "args": ["clippy", "--all-targets", "--all-features", "--",
"-D", "warnings"]
  },
  {
    "label": "test",
    "command": "cargo",
    "args": ["nextest", "run"]
  }
]
```

We can now open the task picker with **`Ctrl + Shift + P`** and select any entry from the list. Our first task rebuilds and reloads LibroCommerce whenever we save a file, and we keep it running throughout every session from this chapter onward. The second reproduces the exact lint gate our pipeline enforces later, so we discover failures locally rather than after pushing. Finally, the third runs our suite through the faster runner installed earlier.

Those of us who prefer VS Code can reach an equivalent setup in two steps. We install the **`rust-analyzer`** extension from the marketplace, then open our workspace settings and set **`rust-analyzer.check.command`** to **`clippy`** alongside **`rust-analyzer.cargo.allFeatures`** to **`true`**, which mirrors the Zed configuration above almost exactly. Every task defined here maps to a plain Cargo command, so nothing in the remaining chapters assumes one editor over the other, and both setups produce identical builds.

Scaffolding LibroCommerce

Generating from 'start-axum-workspace'

The first edition arranged its folders by hand, and that arrangement diverged from how Leptos projects are actually structured in practice. We shall correct that now by generating our project from the official workspace template maintained by the Leptos team. The template hands us a correct build configuration, a working server and client split, and hydration wired up properly, none of which we would enjoy assembling manually or debugging afterwards when a subtle mismatch prevents the browser bundle from mounting.

We will now move to the directory where our projects live and invoke the template through the build tool installed earlier.

```
cargo leptos new --git leptos-rs/start-axum-workspace
```

The generator asks for a project name, and we supply **libro_commerce**. Our project directory appears immediately afterwards, and we then step into it.

```
cd libro_commerce
```

We then add the toolchain pin described earlier, since the template does not supply one and we want our compiler fixed from the very first build.

```
cat > rust-toolchain.toml <<'EOF'
[toolchain]
channel = "1.95.0"
components = ["rustfmt", "clippy", "rust-analyzer"]
targets = ["wasm32-unknown-unknown"]
EOF
```

The next **cargo** command we run inside this directory triggers **rustup** to fetch 1.95.0 whenever our machine lacks it, and every subsequent build then uses that exact compiler. By this point the environment has become reproducible, and any divergence between two machines running LibroCommerce now has to come from somewhere other than the compiler itself, which narrows our search considerably whenever something behaves unexpectedly during the chapters ahead. The compiler has stopped being a variable in that search.

Understanding Workspace Layout

The generated project separates concerns across several crates rather than one, and understanding that separation now prevents confusion for the rest of the book. We will inspect the structure before changing anything at all.

```
ls
```

The template produces a workspace root alongside three member crates and a handful of asset directories.

```
Cargo.toml    app/    frontend/    server/    public/    style/
end2end/
```

The **app** crate holds our shared components, routes, and server functions, and it compiles into both targets. Alongside it, the frontend crate provides the WebAssembly entry point that mounts the application in the browser and does nothing more than that. The **server** crate holds the Axum binary that serves rendered HTML, static assets, and our API. Stylesheets sit under style, static files under public, and browser tests under end2end, which our release pipeline eventually runs on every tagged build.

The relationships between those crates matter rather more than the folder names, and the diagram below traces how our code flows into the two artifacts we ultimately ship.

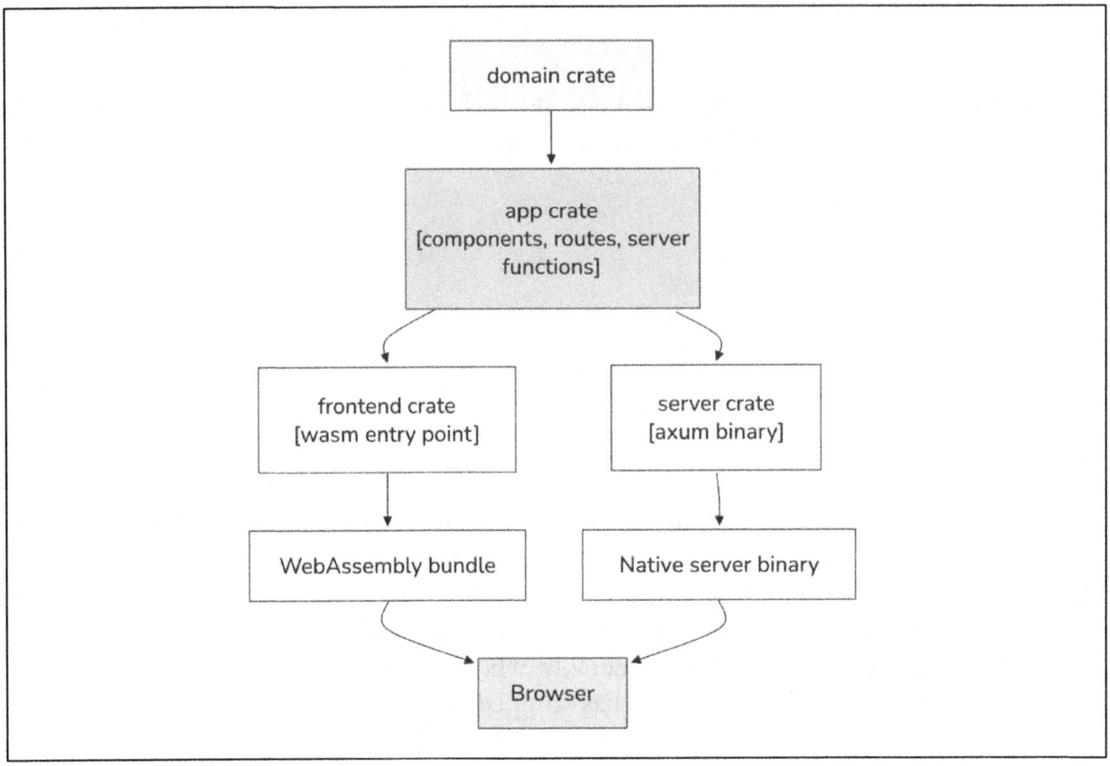

This crate becomes the shared foundation beneath both the Axum backend and the Actix Web backend we build later, and placing it there keeps our business rules entirely independent of whichever framework happens to serve a given request at runtime. That independence becomes the whole point of the second backend.

Locked Dependency Set

We will fix every dependency version in one place so that our chapters stay consistent with one another and with the code accompanying this book. The workspace-level dependency declarations are great because they let member crates inherit versions, rather than restating them. This means that there's no chance of two crates disagreeing about a shared library and producing type errors that make very little sense at first reading.

We then open the workspace manifest.

```
zed Cargo.toml
```

So here, we will then set the package metadata and declare our full dependency set at the workspace level.

```toml
[workspace]
members = ["app", "frontend", "server"]
resolver = "3"

[workspace.package]
version = "0.1.0"
edition = "2024"
rust-version = "1.95"

[workspace.dependencies]
leptos = "0.8.19"
leptos_axum = "0.8.19"
leptos_router = "0.8.19"
axum = "0.8.9"
tokio = { version = "1", features = ["full"] }
tower-http = { version = "0.6.8", features = ["fs", "trace"] }
sqlx = { version = "0.8.6", features = ["runtime-tokio-rustls",
"postgres", "macros", "chrono", "uuid"] }
serde = { version = "1.0", features = ["derive"] }
serde_json = "1.0"
reqwest = { version = "0.12", features = ["json"] }
jsonwebtoken = { version = "10", default-features = false,
features = ["rust_crypto"] }
argon2 = "0.5.3"
oauth2 = "5.0.0"
async-graphql = "7.2.1"
async-graphql-axum = "7.2.1"
redis = { version = "1", features = ["tokio-comp"] }
dotenvy = "0.15"
tracing = "0.1"
tracing-subscriber = { version = "0.3", features = ["env-filter",
"fmt", "json"] }
```

```
uuid = { version = "1", features = ["v4", "serde"] }

chrono = { version = "0.4", features = ["serde"] }
```

A handful of entries carry decisions worth stating plainly. We select **jsonwebtoken** version 10 with the **rust_crypto** backend, because version 9 carries a published security advisory and version 10 requires an explicit backend choice, while the pure Rust option keeps our build free of any system C compiler dependency. sqlx stays at 0.8.6 rather than moving to the newer 0.9 line, since 0.8 has been stable for over a year and the surrounding ecosystem targets it. We also replace the unmaintained **dotenv** crate with **dotenvy**, its maintained successor.

The **rust-version** field works together with **resolver = "3"**, which the 2024 edition enables for us automatically. Whenever Cargo resolves dependencies, it consults that field, and it then declines to select any release demanding a compiler newer than 1.95. This project therefore keeps building even as the crates we depend upon raise their own minimum requirements over the coming months, which is precisely the failure mode that stranded so much of the first edition once its dependencies moved on.

Running Postgres and Redis

LibroCommerce stores its catalogue, users, and orders in PostgreSQL, and it keeps sessions in Redis once we harden the application later. We are going to run both as containers rather than installing them system-wide, so that our versions match this book exactly, and we can reset our data at any moment without disturbing anything else on the machine. A container image pins the database version as firmly as **rust-toolchain.toml** pins our compiler, and both forms of pinning serve exactly the same purpose.

In the script below, we will now install Docker Engine from the distribution repositories and add ourselves to the **docker** group.

```
sudo apt update && sudo apt install -y docker.io docker-compose-v2

sudo usermod -aG docker "$USER"
```

That group membership takes effect on the next login, so we log out and back in before continuing, otherwise every Docker command asks for elevated privileges. We shall then describe both services in a compose file placed at our project root, where the definition sits alongside the code that depends upon it and travels with the repository whenever somebody clones LibroCommerce for the first time.

Both services then start together from a single command, and neither one needs any manual configuration afterwards.

```
services:

  postgres:
```

```yaml
    image: postgres:17
    container_name: libro_postgres
    environment:
      POSTGRES_USER: libro
      POSTGRES_PASSWORD: libro_dev_password
      POSTGRES_DB: libro_commerce
    ports:
      - "5432:5432"
    volumes:
      - libro_pgdata:/var/lib/postgresql/data
    healthcheck:
      test: ["CMD-SHELL", "pg_isready -U libro -d
libro_commerce"]
      interval: 5s
      retries: 5

  redis:
    image: redis:8
    container_name: libro_redis
    ports:
      - "6379:6379"
    volumes:
      - libro_redisdata:/data

volumes:
  libro_pgdata:
  libro_redisdata:
```

We can now bring both services up in the background.

```
docker compose up -d
```

The daemon pulls each image on first run and then reports the state of every container it has created.

```
[+] Running 4/4
 ✓ Network libro_commerce_default  Created
 ✓ Volume libro_pgdata             Created
 ✓ Container libro_postgres        Healthy
 ✓ Container libro_redis           Started
```

The app reads its connection details from environment variables rather than from hardcoded strings, and we will now record those variables so that our database layer can pick them up later without any further setup. And, the named volumes declared above keep our data alive across container restarts, while a **`docker compose down -v`** wipes them completely whenever we want a clean database to work against. That reset costs us seconds rather than a full reinstallation of the database server.

```
cat > .env <<'EOF'
DATABASE_URL=postgres://libro:libro_dev_password@localhost:5432/l
ibro_commerce
REDIS_URL=redis://localhost:6379
RUST_LOG=info,libro_commerce=debug
EOF
```

Initializing Git and Committing 'Cargo.lock'

Our project needs version control from the very first commit, and the template has already placed a **`.gitignore`** that excludes build artifacts. We will now initialize the repository and record our starting state.

```
git init
git add .
git commit -m "Scaffold LibroCommerce from start-axum-workspace"
```

A single file in that commit carries disproportionate weight, and we should be explicit about why. The **`cargo.lock`** file records the exact resolved version of every direct and transitive dependency, and committing it converts our project from "whichever compatible versions Cargo picks today" into "the exact versions this book was written against". Whoever clones LibroCommerce afterwards receives an identical dependency graph, and the ecosystem drift that breaks older projects simply cannot reach us.

We shall now adopt a simple branching arrangement that carries us through the remaining chapters. The main branch always holds working code, and we develop each chapter on its own branch before merging it back.

```
git checkout -b chapter-01
```

Every chapter afterwards follows the same pattern, so Chapter 2 begins on chapter-02 branched from main. A branch per chapter lets us return to any earlier state without difficulty, and it mirrors how feature work actually proceeds on a real team. Each commit also gives us a natural checkpoint whenever an experiment goes wrong, which happens often enough while learning an unfamiliar framework that the habit repays itself very quickly.

Building "Hello, LibroCommerce!"

Writing Leptos Component

We will now replace the template's placeholder interface with the first piece of LibroCommerce, and we keep that first piece deliberately small so the build pipeline stays the subject rather than the markup. That shared crate holds the component tree, so we open its library file for editing. Whatever we place there compiles into both the server binary and the browser bundle, which is precisely why the shared crate exists.

```
zed app/src/lib.rs
```

So here, we will then locate the existing **App** component and rewrite it as a greeting that names our application and proves reactivity is working.

```
use leptos::prelude::*;


#[component]

pub fn App() -> impl IntoView {

    let (visits, set_visits) = signal(0);


    view! {

        <main class="container">

            <h1>"Hello, LibroCommerce!"</h1>

            <p>"Our storefront is running on Rust, Axum and
Leptos."</p>
```

```
            <button on:click=move |_| set_visits.update(|n| *n +=
1)>
                "Browsed " {move || visits.get()} " times"
            </button>
        </main>
    }
}
```

That component introduces the reactive primitive we rely on throughout our front-end work. A call to **signal** returns a getter alongside a setter, and any part of our view that reads the getter re-renders automatically whenever the setter runs. The closure inside the braces creates that subscription, while the click handler updates the value. At no point does virtual DOM diffing take place, because Leptos updates only the specific DOM node depending on that signal.

Compiling to WebAssembly

We will now build and serve our application through the Leptos build tool, which watches our files and rebuilds whenever we save. That Zed task configured earlier runs exactly this command, though we invoke it directly the first time so that we can observe the full build as it happens and recognize each stage when it later scrolls past inside the editor panel. The tool also opens a websocket to our browser, so that saved changes appear without any manual refresh.

```
cargo leptos watch
```

The first build takes several minutes, because Cargo compiles the entire dependency graph twice, once for the native server target and once for WebAssembly. Every build after that finishes in seconds, since only our changed crates recompile. The tool reports each stage as it proceeds and then confirms that the server has started listening on the port it selected for us.

```
   Compiling libro_commerce_app v0.1.0
   Compiling libro_commerce_frontend v0.1.0
   Compiling libro_commerce_server v0.1.0
    Finished `dev` profile in 218.44s
      Serving at http://127.0.0.1:3000
```

The sequence behind that output involves rather more moving parts than a conventional web build, and the diagram below traces what the tool does on our behalf each time we save a file.

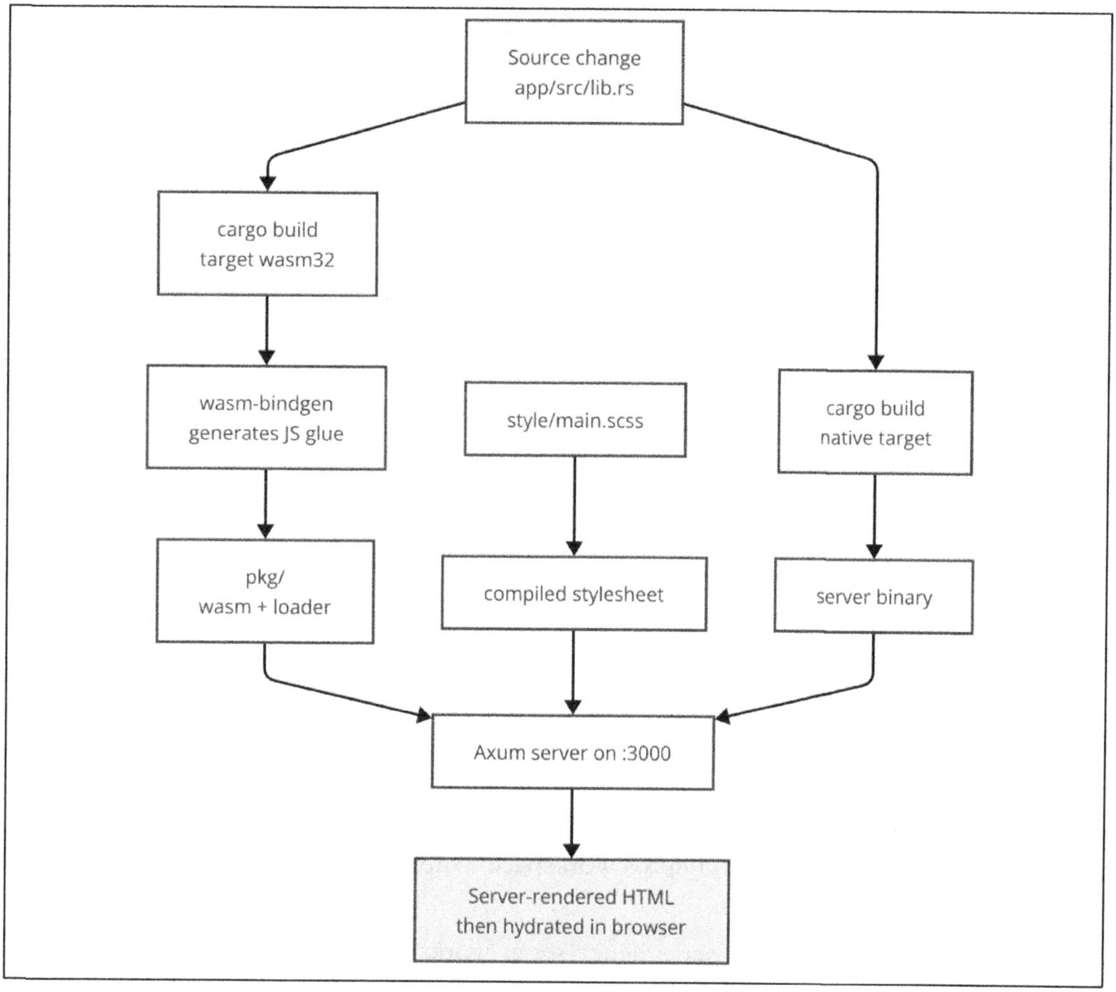

A pair of artifacts reaches the browser on every request. The server renders the initial HTML so the page appears immediately, and search engines receive real content, then the WebAssembly bundle loads and attaches event handlers to the markup already present. That second step carries the name hydration, and we work through its implications in considerable detail later, once our interface grows beyond a single greeting.

Verifying in Browser

We can now open a browser and visit the address our server reported, namely **`http://127.0.0.1:3000`**. That greeting appears alongside the button we defined, and clicking that button increments the tally without any page reload and without any JavaScript that we wrote ourselves. The increment happens inside compiled Rust running as WebAssembly, which makes this small page a genuine demonstration of the full stack rather than a placeholder we discard later. Every layer of the stack is now demonstrably working from end to end.

We shall then confirm that hydration is working correctly by disabling JavaScript in our browser and reloading the page. Both the heading and the paragraph still render, because the server produced them, while the button stops responding, because its behaviour lives in the WebAssembly bundle that never loaded. That contrast shows precisely which parts of LibroCommerce depend on the client and which parts survive without it, and we return to that distinction whenever we weigh server-side rendering against client interactivity.

Meanwhile, we can commit our work and merge the chapter branch back into **`main`**.

```
git add .

git commit -m "Add LibroCommerce greeting component and local
services"

git checkout main

git merge chapter-01
```

Summary

We built the foundation that every remaining chapter stands upon. The toolchain now sits pinned at Rust 1.95.0 through rust-toolchain.toml, so the compiler, formatter, linter, and WebAssembly target install themselves identically for anyone cloning our project. We adopted the 2024 edition, paired it with **`resolver = "3"`** and a declared **`rust-version`**, configured Zed with continuous Clippy feedback and committed project tasks, and generated LibroCommerce from the official Leptos workspace template rather than arranging folders by hand as the first edition did.

We then declared our complete dependency set at workspace level, brought PostgreSQL 17 and Redis 8 up as containers, and committed **`Cargo.lock`** so that our dependency graph stays fixed rather than drifting over time. That first Leptos component now compiles for two targets at once and behaves correctly in the browser. In the next chapter, we take this workspace and give it a proper architecture, where we add the domain crate sketched in our diagram and establish the observability layer that carries us onward.

CHAPTER 2

DESIGNING MODERN ARCHITECTURE

We will now give the workspace generated in the previous chapter a proper architecture, and that work centres on one addition we already promised, namely the shared **`domain`** crate. Our aim throughout this chapter involves separating what LibroCommerce actually does from the framework that happens to deliver it, so that our business rules live in a single place and stay entirely independent of Axum, of Actix Web, and of the browser itself. That separation forms the whole subject of this chapter.

We are going to model our books, users, and orders as plain Rust types, express our service boundaries as traits, define one error type that crosses those boundaries cleanly, and establish the tracing layer that carries diagnostic information through every later chapter. From this chapter, our workspace is going to hold a compilable architecture with no handlers and no database attached to it, which is precisely the point of the exercise. In the next chapter, we then fit a web server around it.

Modern Web Architecture

Microservices for Modern Apps

I will be very candid about terminology before adopting it. A microservice architecture, if taken strictly, deploys each service area as an independent process with its own database and its own release cycle. Our application does not need that, and neither do most applications of its size. What we borrow instead is the discipline behind the pattern, where each service area owns its data, exposes a narrow interface, and never reaches into another area's internals. Those modules therefore stay separable without paying the considerable operational cost that real separation demands.

That distinction matters practically rather than academically. When our inventory logic depends only on an **`InventoryService`** trait, we can replace its storage layer, test it against an in-memory fake, or eventually extract it into a standalone binary without touching any code that calls it. Those options stay open because of how we draw the boundaries today, and none of them require us to run three deployments from the outset. We therefore gain the flexibility while deferring the complexity until something in production actually demands it of us.

Three service areas fall out naturally from the application itself:

1. The inventory area owns the catalogue, stock levels, and book metadata.
2. The orders area owns carts, order lines, payment state, and the lifecycle an order moves through.
3. And, the accounts area owns users, credentials, and sessions.

Each area touches the others only through well-defined operations, so an order confirms stock by asking inventory rather than by querying the books table directly, and that single rule prevents most of the tangling that makes older applications so difficult to change safely.

Key Architectural Patterns

A pair of patterns shapes everything that follows, and both are worth naming explicitly. The first involves dependency inversion, where our high-level logic depends on abstractions rather than on concrete implementations. That crate defines traits and knows nothing about PostgreSQL, HTTP, or WebAssembly. The crates that do know about those technologies depend on **`domain`** instead of the reverse, so our dependency arrows all point inward toward the code that changes least often across the life of the application.

The second pattern concerns the shared kernel, where one crate holds the types that every other crate agrees upon. Those Book, Order, and User types compile into the server binary and into the WebAssembly bundle alike, so a field we rename in domain produces compile errors in both places at once rather than a runtime mismatch discovered by a visitor. That property alone justifies the whole arrangement, because a frontend and a backend drifting quietly apart is among the most common failures in web development.

Both patterns pay off directly once a second backend arrives. That second backend will consume the very same traits and the very same models as the first, and neither backend contains a single line of business logic. Each one translates HTTP into domain operations and translates domain results back into HTTP responses, which is the entirety of its job. A framework swap therefore becomes a question of rewriting the translation layer rather than the application, and that is exactly the outcome we want.

Structuring Cargo Workspace

Creating Shared Domain Crate

We will now create the crate that holds our application logic, and Cargo generates its skeleton for us.

```
cargo new --lib domain
```

We then register the crate as a workspace member and declare the two additions our domain layer needs. For this, we open the workspace manifest and extend the sections established earlier.

```
[workspace]
members = ["app", "domain", "frontend", "server-axum"]
resolver = "3"

[workspace.dependencies]
domain = { path = "domain" }
```

```
thiserror = "2"
```

The **`thiserror`** crate generates the boilerplate that a well-behaved error type requires, and it adds nothing at all at runtime because its work happens entirely at compile time. That domain entry lets every other member depend on the crate by name rather than by a repeated relative path, which keeps the individual manifests short and consistent. We shall then declare the dependencies our domain crate itself requires, all of which inherit their versions from the workspace rather than restating them.

```
[package]
name = "domain"
version.workspace = true
edition.workspace = true
rust-version.workspace = true

[dependencies]
serde = { workspace = true }
uuid = { workspace = true }
chrono = { workspace = true }
thiserror = { workspace = true }
tracing = { workspace = true }
```

What that list omits matters more than what it contains. Nowhere within it does a web framework, a database driver, or an asynchronous runtime appear. That crate compiles to WebAssembly and to native code equally well, precisely because it depends on nothing that is specific to either environment.

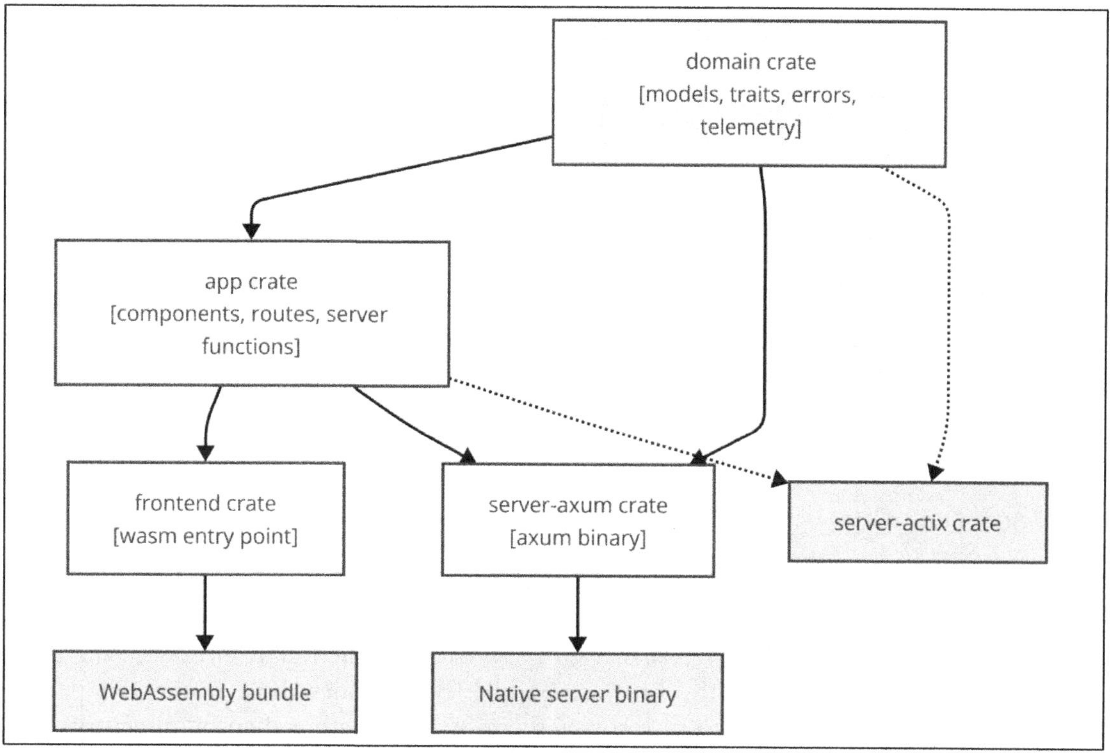

Renaming Server Crate

The template produced a crate named server, and that name serves us poorly the moment a second backend arrives. We shall rename it now, while exactly one crate depends upon it, rather than later, when the same rename would touch considerably more code and risk breaking work in progress. A rename grows more expensive as a project matures, so we pay this particular cost at the cheapest possible moment. The version history records the change as a rename rather than as a deletion followed by an addition.

```
git mv server server-axum
```

Once this is in place, we open the crate manifest and change the package name to match its new location, adding the domain dependency at the same time.

```
[package]
name = "server-axum"
version.workspace = true
edition.workspace = true
rust-version.workspace = true
```

```
[dependencies]
app = { path = "../app", features = ["ssr"] }
domain = { workspace = true }
axum = { workspace = true }
leptos = { workspace = true }
leptos_axum = { workspace = true }
tokio = { workspace = true }
tower-http = { workspace = true }
tracing = { workspace = true }
tracing-subscriber = { workspace = true }
```

The build tool still points at the old package name, so a third adjustment updates the Leptos metadata our template generated. We change the binary package entry inside the workspace manifest, since **cargo leptos** reads that entry to decide which crate produces the server executable and which produces the browser bundle. Both values must match our package names exactly, because the build tool resolves them by name rather than by directory, and a mismatch here produces an error that mentions neither crate clearly.

```
[[workspace.metadata.leptos]]
name = "libro_commerce"
bin-package = "server-axum"
lib-package = "frontend"
```

We can now confirm that the workspace still resolves correctly after all three changes.

```
cargo check --workspace
```

Every member compiles under that command while Cargo reports the outcome, and a clean run here tells us the rename propagated everywhere it needed to reach.

```
    Checking domain v0.1.0
    Checking app v0.1.0
    Checking server-axum v0.1.0
    Finished `dev` profile in 12.83s
```

Feature Flags and Conditional Compilation

Both backends will share the app crate, and that crate therefore needs some way to know which framework integration it should compile against. That's exactly what feature flags in Cargo do, because they let you switch a set of optional dependencies and conditional code on or off.

We shall now establish the pattern with a single backend, so that our second backend extends something familiar rather than inventing an arrangement from nothing.

```
[features]
default = []
hydrate = ["leptos/hydrate"]
ssr = ["leptos/ssr", "dep:domain"]
backend-axum = ["ssr", "dep:leptos_axum"]

[dependencies]
leptos = { workspace = true }
leptos_router = { workspace = true }
serde = { workspace = true }
domain = { workspace = true, optional = true }
leptos_axum = { workspace = true, optional = true }
```

In the above, the **dep:** prefix names an optional dependency and enables it, while a bare feature name enables another feature of our own crate. The backend-axum feature therefore turns on ssr first, which brings in the domain crate along with server-side rendering, and then adds the Axum integration on top of that foundation. They compose rather than conflict, which is what makes the arrangement extensible.

The source reads those features through conditional compilation attributes, and the pattern below appears throughout the chapters ahead whenever framework-specific code needs isolating.

```
#[cfg(feature = "backend-axum")]
pub mod axum_integration;

#[cfg(feature = "backend-actix")]
pub mod actix_integration;
```

```
#[cfg(feature = "ssr")]
pub fn domain_available() -> bool {
    true
}
```

Every module guarded that way disappears entirely from builds where its feature stays off, so our WebAssembly bundle never carries server code and our server never carries hydration code. That separation keeps our browser payload small, which matters directly for the load times we tune later. This arrangement also means a mistake inside the Actix integration cannot break the Axum build, because the compiler never sees the offending module at all.

Defining Service Boundaries

Modelling Inventory, Orders and Accounts

We will now express our three service areas as Rust types, and every type we write derives the traits that let it cross the wire in either direction. These models live inside a dedicated module in the domain crate, so we create that file first and describe the catalogue before anything else. The book type forms the foundation, since orders reference it and the storefront displays it.

```
use chrono::{DateTime, Utc};
use serde::{Deserialize, Serialize};
use uuid::Uuid;

#[derive(Debug, Clone, PartialEq, Serialize, Deserialize)]
pub struct Book {
    pub id: Uuid,
    pub isbn: String,
    pub title: String,
    pub author: String,
    pub price_cents: i64,
    pub stock: i32,
    pub published_on: DateTime<Utc>,
}
```

```
#[derive(Debug, Clone, Default, Serialize, Deserialize)]
pub struct BookFilter {
    pub author: Option<String>,
    pub search: Option<String>,
    pub in_stock_only: bool,
    pub limit: i64,
    pub offset: i64,
}
```

From the above, we store money as **`price_cents`** rather than as a floating-point value, because binary floating point cannot represent most decimal amounts exactly and those rounding errors accumulate across the lines of an order. The BookFilter type gathers every catalogue query parameter into a single struct, which keeps the trait signature stable as we add further filters later.

The order model carries rather more structure, since an order holds lines and moves through a lifecycle. So here, we shall define those types alongside the status enumeration that governs the lifecycle.

```
#[derive(Debug, Clone, Copy, PartialEq, Eq, Serialize,
Deserialize)]
#[serde(rename_all = "snake_case")]
pub enum OrderStatus {
    Pending,
    Paid,
    Packed,
    Shipped,
    Delivered,
    Cancelled,
}

#[derive(Debug, Clone, PartialEq, Serialize, Deserialize)]
pub struct OrderLine {
    pub book_id: Uuid,
    pub quantity: i32,
```

```
    pub unit_price_cents: i64,
}

#[derive(Debug, Clone, PartialEq, Serialize, Deserialize)]
pub struct Order {
    pub id: Uuid,
    pub user_id: Uuid,
    pub lines: Vec<OrderLine>,
    pub status: OrderStatus,
    pub placed_at: DateTime<Utc>,
}

#[derive(Debug, Clone, PartialEq, Serialize, Deserialize)]
pub struct User {
    pub id: Uuid,
    pub email: String,
    pub display_name: String,
    pub created_at: DateTime<Utc>,
}
```

The OrderLine type records unit_price_cents rather than reading the current price from the catalogue, and that choice is entirely deliberate. A price change tomorrow must never alter what a visitor paid today, so the order captures the price at the exact moment of purchase and keeps it. The relationships between all four types appear below:

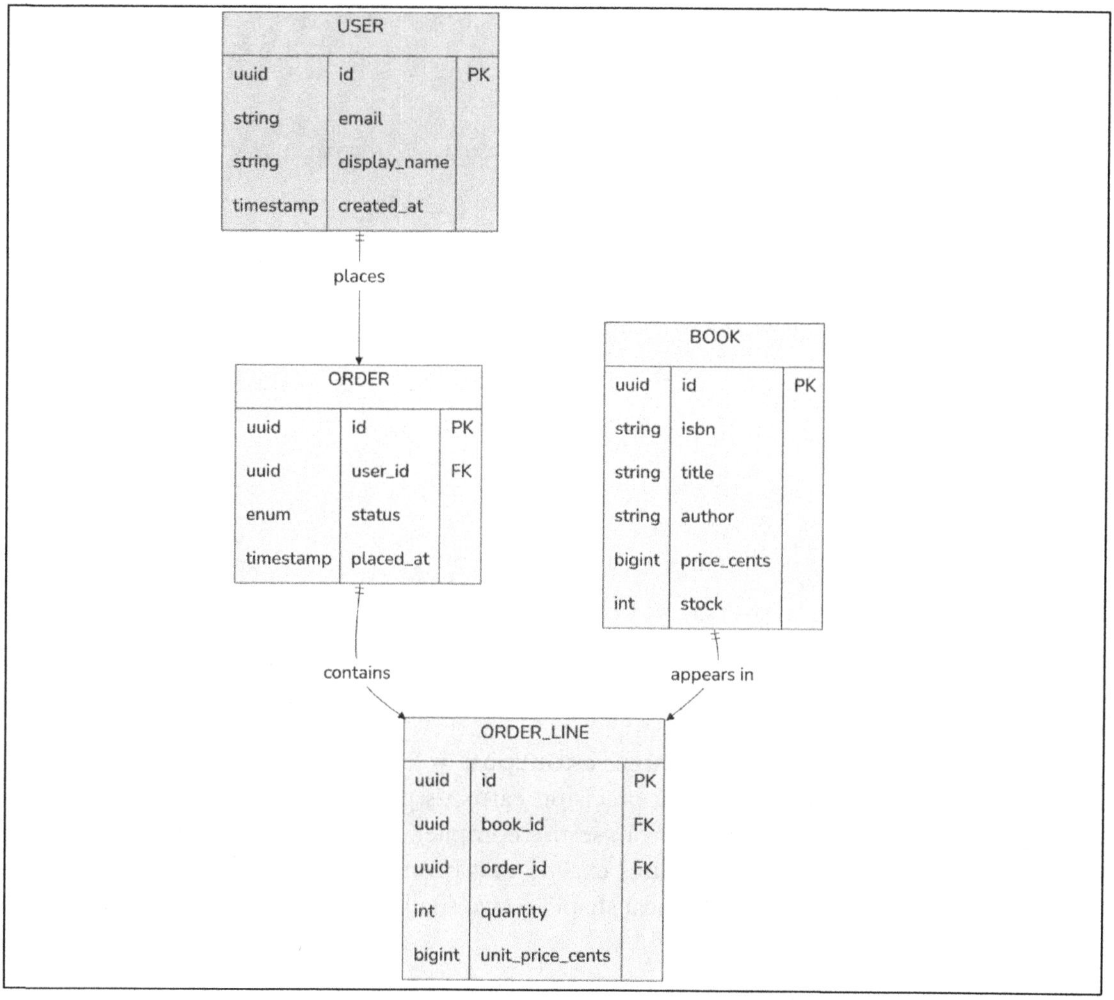

Writing Service Traits

We are now ready to describe what each service area can actually do, and traits give us that description without committing to any implementation whatsoever. These traits use asynchronous methods, since every operation eventually touches a database or a network. The good thing about asynchronous functions inside traits is that they're supported directly, but we do have to write the return type explicitly so that our futures carry a Send bound. This means they can move between threads on the Tokio runtime.

```
use std::future::Future;

use uuid::Uuid;


use crate::error::DomainError;
```

```
use crate::models::{Book, BookFilter, Order, OrderLine,
OrderStatus, User};

pub trait InventoryService: Send + Sync + 'static {
    fn list_books(&self, filter: BookFilter)
        -> impl Future<Output = Result<Vec<Book>, DomainError>> +
Send;

    fn find_book(&self, id: Uuid)
        -> impl Future<Output = Result<Book, DomainError>> +
Send;

    fn reserve_stock(&self, id: Uuid, quantity: i32)
        -> impl Future<Output = Result<Book, DomainError>> +
Send;
}
```

From the above, the explicit **impl Future<Output = ...> + Send** reads more heavily than a plain **async fn**, and the extra precision earns its place. Without that bound, a caller holding our trait generically cannot promise the compiler that the resulting future is safe to move across threads, and Axum requires exactly that promise from every handler it accepts. Both remaining traits follow the identical shape, so we shall then define the order and account boundaries in turn.

```
pub trait OrderService: Send + Sync + 'static {
    fn place_order(&self, user_id: Uuid, lines: Vec<OrderLine>)
        -> impl Future<Output = Result<Order, DomainError>> +
Send;

    fn find_order(&self, id: Uuid)
        -> impl Future<Output = Result<Order, DomainError>> +
Send;

    fn advance_status(&self, id: Uuid, next: OrderStatus)
        -> impl Future<Output = Result<Order, DomainError>> +
Send;
```

```
}


pub trait AccountService: Send + Sync + 'static {
    fn register(&self, email: String, display_name: String,
password: String)
        -> impl Future<Output = Result<User, DomainError>> +
Send;


    fn authenticate(&self, email: String, password: String)
        -> impl Future<Output = Result<User, DomainError>> +
Send;
}
```

The **advance_status** method deserves a closer look, because it enforces a rule rather than merely writing a value into storage. An order may move from Pending to Paid, yet it must never move from Delivered back to Pending, and our implementation later rejects any transition the lifecycle forbids. We place that rule inside the domain rather than inside a handler, so both backends inherit it automatically, and the diagram below records exactly which transitions we permit.

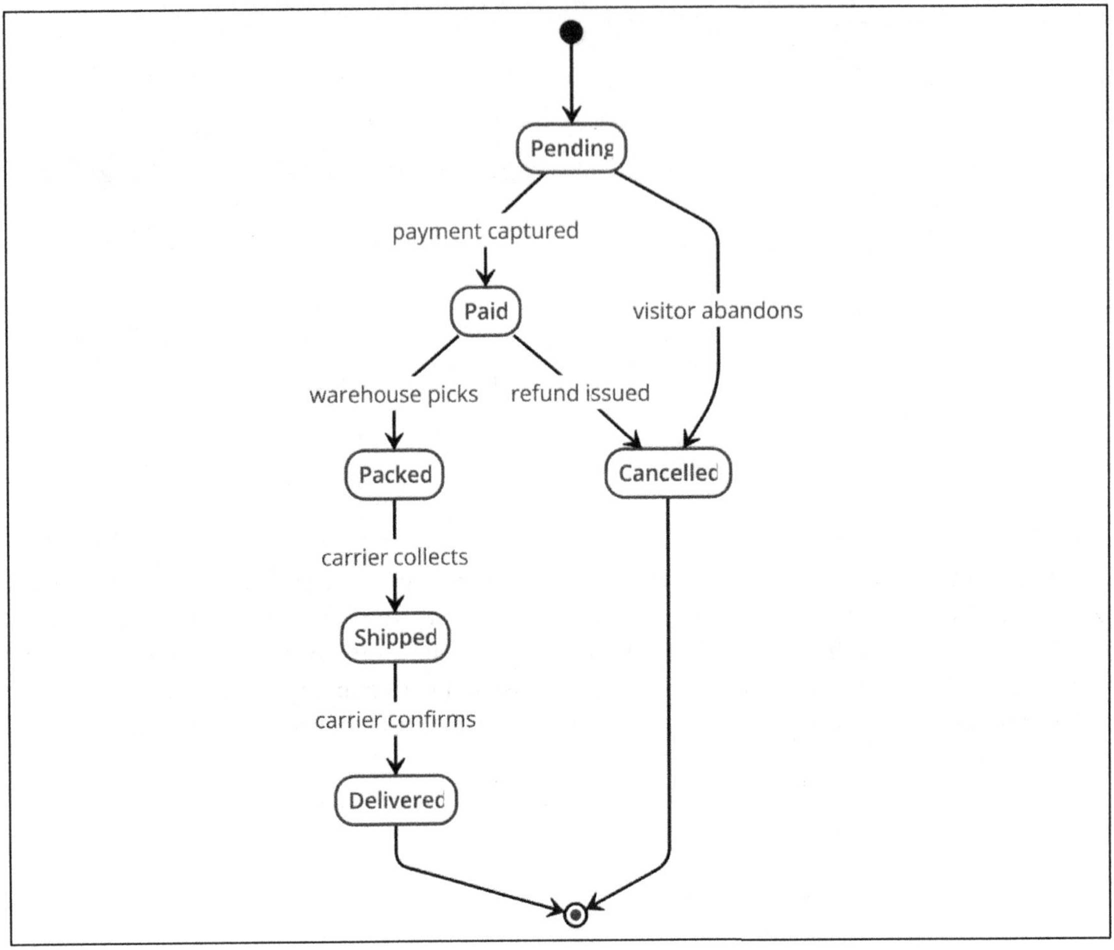

Defining Domain Error Type

Every method above returns the same error type, and that consistency is well worth the small effort it costs us. A single error type means our handlers translate failures into HTTP responses in one place rather than in dozens of scattered locations, and it means adding a new failure mode later updates one enumeration instead of spreading changes across the whole application. Every caller is also forced to handle each new variant, so nothing slips past unnoticed. We shall now define that type inside the domain crate.

```
use uuid::Uuid;

use crate::models::OrderStatus;

#[derive(Debug, thiserror::Error)]
```

```
pub enum DomainError {
    #[error("book {0} was not found")]
    BookNotFound(Uuid),

    #[error("order {0} was not found")]
    OrderNotFound(Uuid),

    #[error("only {available} copies of book {id} remain in
stock")]
    InsufficientStock { id: Uuid, available: i32 },

    #[error("order {order} cannot move from {from:?} to {to:?}")]
    InvalidTransition { order: Uuid, from: OrderStatus, to:
OrderStatus },

    #[error("the supplied credentials were rejected")]
    InvalidCredentials,

    #[error("a storage operation failed")]
    Storage(#[source] Box<dyn std::error::Error + Send + Sync>),
}
```

Each variant carries the data a caller needs in order to react sensibly. Our **InsufficientStock** variant reports how many copies remain, so a frontend can display that number rather than a generic apology that helps nobody. The **Storage** variant wraps any underlying failure behind a boxed source, which keeps database-specific error types out of our domain crate while preserving the original cause for our logs. In the next chapter, we map each variant onto an appropriate status code inside the web layer.

The domain crate also needs a module list. So here, we complete it by declaring every module and re-exporting the type that callers reach for most often.

```
pub mod error;
pub mod models;
pub mod services;
```

```
pub mod telemetry;

pub use error::DomainError;
```

Mapping Data Flows across Stack

Tracing End-to-End Request Path

We should follow a single request through every layer before writing any more code, because that walkthrough reveals whether our boundaries actually hold under pressure. The example we choose involves a visitor opening a book detail view, which touches the browser, our server, the domain traits, and eventually the database itself. Each hop crosses exactly one boundary, and no layer reaches past its immediate neighbour to shortcut the path. That walkthrough therefore doubles as a check on the design itself.

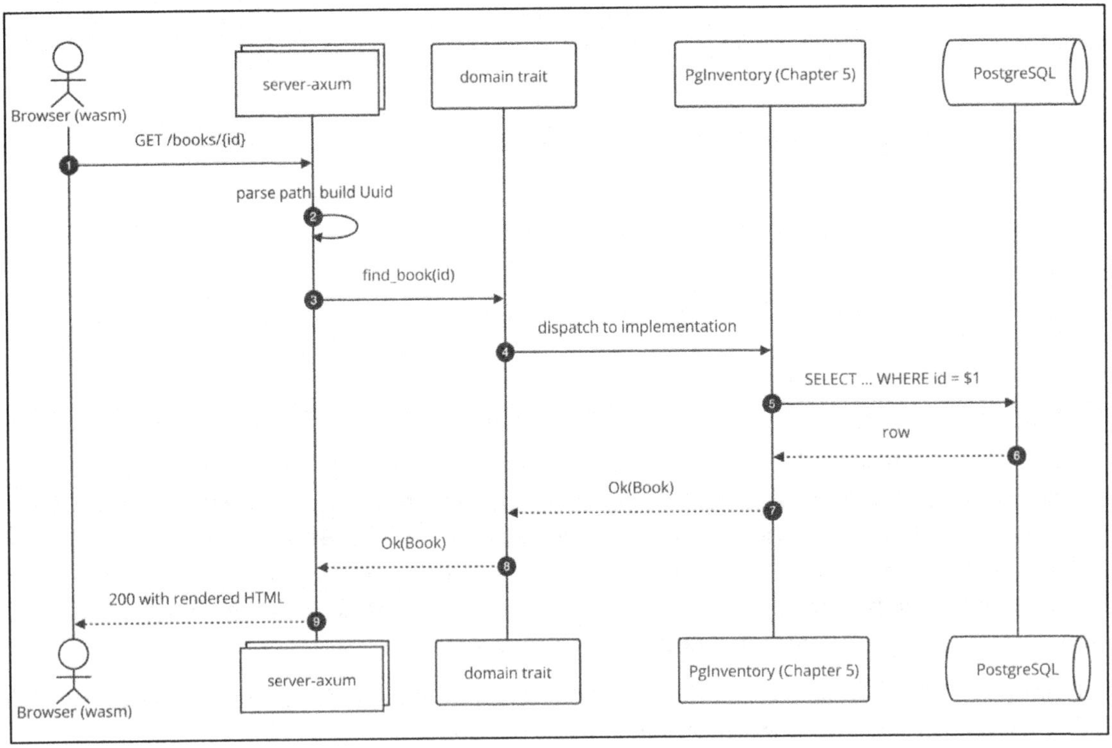

A pair of properties in the above diagram matters rather more than the individual steps. That server-axum layer never constructs a SQL query and never knows that PostgreSQL exists, while our PgInventory implementation never knows that HTTP exists at all. You can't accidentally depend on the two layers together because the domain trait sits between them and the compiler enforces that separation for us. A replacement at either end therefore leaves the opposite end completely untouched, which is what allows us to swap frameworks later.

The same path runs in reverse whenever something fails. A missing row produces **DomainError::BookNotFound**, that value travels back through the trait entirely unchanged, and our web layer converts it into a 404 response at the very last moment. And below the handler, the layers don't know anything about status codes. The same goes for above the implementation, where the layers don't know anything about database rows. Error handling therefore stays as clean as the success path, which very rarely happens by accident.

Pairing Server Functions with Components

There is a mechanism in Leptos that fits our architecture unusually well, namely the server function. A function annotated as such compiles into our server binary as a real endpoint and into our WebAssembly bundle as a typed remote call, so our components invoke it exactly as they would invoke any asynchronous function. These domain types cross that boundary directly, since both sides of the call share the same Book definition drawn from the domain crate.

```
use leptos::prelude::*;


#[server(ListBooks, "/api")]
pub async fn list_books(filter: BookFilter) -> Result<Vec<Book>,
ServerFnError> {
    use crate::state::inventory;
    inventory()
        .list_books(filter)
        .await
        .map_err(|e| ServerFnError::new(e.to_string()))
}
```

That single function replaces a hand-written REST endpoint, a client-side fetch call, and the serialization code on both sides of the wire. The macro generates the route, the request encoding, and the response decoding, while our body simply delegates to the domain trait. Our component layer therefore stays free of transport concerns entirely, and a change to **BookFilter** breaks compilation on both sides at once rather than producing a mismatch that only surfaces at runtime.

We should be clear about where server functions stop being appropriate, because they are certainly not a universal replacement. An interface consumed by something other than our own frontend still needs an explicit endpoint, which is precisely why we build REST and GraphQL surfaces alongside these functions later. As a rule of thumb, server functions serve internal calls between our own components and our own server, while public interfaces get designed and versioned deliberately.

Logging and Observability

Initializing Tracing Subscriber

We will now establish the diagnostic layer that every later chapter depends upon, and we place it inside the domain crate so that both backends share exactly one configuration. The **tracing** crate separates the recording of events from their processing, where our code emits structured events and a subscriber then decides what to do with them. That subscriber reads its filtering rules from the **RUST_LOG** variable we placed inside the .env file earlier. We need no recompilation whenever we change them.

```
use tracing_subscriber::{fmt, EnvFilter};


pub fn init_tracing(json_output: bool) {
    let filter = EnvFilter::try_from_default_env()
        .unwrap_or_else(|_| EnvFilter::new("info"));


    let builder = fmt()
        .with_env_filter(filter)
        .with_target(true)
        .with_file(true)
        .with_line_number(true);


    if json_output {
        builder.json().init();
    } else {
        builder.pretty().init();
    }
}
```

The function takes a flag rather than deciding for itself, because the two output formats serve quite different situations. A pretty format stays readable while we develop locally, whereas a

JSON format lets a log aggregator in production parse every field without any fragile pattern matching. The same binary therefore produces human output on our machine and machine output in production, and that decision arrives through configuration rather than through a separate rebuild.

Instrumenting Service Methods

The **tracing** crate offers an attribute that wraps any function in a span automatically, recording its arguments, its duration, and its eventual result. We can apply that attribute to our service implementations rather than to the trait definitions, since a trait describes a contract while an implementation performs the actual work.

```
use tracing::instrument;


impl InventoryService for PgInventory {
    #[instrument(skip(self), fields(book_count))]
    async fn list_books(&self, filter: BookFilter) ->
Result<Vec<Book>, DomainError> {
        let books = self.query_books(&filter).await?;
        tracing::Span::current().record("book_count",
books.len());
        tracing::debug!(?filter, "catalogue query completed");
        Ok(books)
    }
}
```

In the above script, the **skip(self)** argument prevents our entire connection pool from being written into every log line, which would be both useless and enormous. The **fields(book_count)** declaration reserves a slot that we populate once the result becomes known, so a single span carries both the inputs and the outcome together. A span opened inside this one nests automatically, and that nesting lets us follow one request through several layers without threading an identifier through every signature by hand.

Reporting Errors through Tracing

The error type already carries enough information to diagnose a failure, so the remaining task involves recording it at the appropriate level. We record expected failures at **warn** and unexpected failures at **error**, because a visitor requesting a deleted book is entirely normal while a database timeout is not. A conflation of the two produces alert fatigue, where genuine incidents disappear inside a steady stream of routine events that nobody reads.

```
use tracing::{error, warn};

pub fn report(err: &DomainError) {
    match err {
        DomainError::Storage(source) => {
            error!(cause = %source, "storage operation failed");
        }
        DomainError::InvalidTransition { order, from, to } => {
            warn!(%order, ?from, ?to, "rejected an invalid order
transition");
        }
        other => {
            warn!(error = %other, "domain rule rejected the
request");
        }
    }
}
```

A pair of sigils appears in those macros, and the two behave differently from one another. The `%` prefix records the value through its **`Display`** implementation, producing readable output, while a **`?`** prefix records it through **`Debug`** and preserves the underlying structure. The choice between them depends on whether a person or a query will read the field later on. Later, we build on these same events when we expose metrics, so the effort we invest here compounds rather than staying local.

We can now confirm that the whole workspace compiles with our new architecture in place.

```
cargo check --workspace --all-features
```

A clean build across every member crate tells us that our traits, models, and error type all agree with one another.

```
    Checking domain v0.1.0
    Checking app v0.1.0
    Checking server-axum v0.1.0
    Checking frontend v0.1.0
```

```
    Finished `dev` profile in 18.02s
```

Summary

We gave LibroCommerce an architecture that separates business rules from delivery mechanics. This new domain crate holds the models, service traits, error type, and telemetry setup, and it depends on no web framework, no database driver, and no asynchronous runtime whatsoever. We renamed the server crate to **`server-axum`** while that rename remained cheap, established the feature-flag mechanism that Chapter 4 extends with a second backend, and confirmed that every member crate still compiles together cleanly.

We then modelled inventory, orders, and accounts as plain Rust types, expressed each service area as a trait returning explicitly bounded futures, and defined one error enumeration that crosses every boundary in the application. The tracing layer now records structured spans around service methods and distinguishes expected failures from genuine incidents. In Chapter 3, we fit an Axum server around this architecture, where handlers translate HTTP into the domain operations we defined and translate domain errors back into status codes.

CHAPTER 3
BUILDING APP SERVER WITH AXUM

We will now fit a web server around the architecture established earlier, and every handler we write does exactly one job, namely translating HTTP into a domain operation and translating the result back into a response. That crate gains routes, application state, error mapping, an outbound integration with a third-party catalogue, and the authentication layer that protects anything belonging to a particular visitor. Every piece we add connects straight back to the domain crate we built.

We are going to work against an in-memory implementation of our inventory trait rather than a database, which lets us build and exercise the entire web layer before PostgreSQL arrives. That substitution costs us nothing and proves the value of the trait boundary immediately, since we later swap the implementation without touching a single handler. With Axum 0.8, both the path syntax and the startup interface changed, so we cover each of those carefully.

Building Responsive Server

Routing in Axum 0.8

We should address one change before writing any routes, because it breaks almost every Axum example published before 2025. A path parameter now uses braces rather than a leading colon, so a route that once read /books/:id becomes /books/{id} instead. The same rule governs wildcard segments, where /assets/*path becomes /assets/{*path}. A route still carrying the older form panics at startup with a message about an invalid path, so the failure surfaces immediately rather than silently. The upgrade therefore fails loudly and early.

Our reasoning behind the change comes from consistency with the wider ecosystem, since OpenAPI, most templating systems, and several sibling frameworks already used braces. The new form also removes a genuine ambiguity, because a colon carries meaning inside a URL, while a brace does not. We shall now declare the routes LibroCommerce needs, keeping every path under an **`/api`** prefix so that our Leptos page routes and our interface never collide with one another. That prefix also simplifies our deployment rules considerably later.

```
use axum::routing::{get, post};

use axum::Router;


pub fn api_routes() -> Router<AppState> {

    Router::new()

        .route("/api/books", get(list_books))

        .route("/api/books/{id}", get(find_book))

        .route("/api/orders", post(place_order))

        .route("/api/orders/{id}", get(find_order))
```

```
        .route("/api/orders/{id}/status", post(advance_status))
        .route("/api/auth/login", post(login))
}
```

That function returns Router<AppState> rather than a plain Router, and that generic parameter matters considerably more than it appears to. A router carrying a state type has not yet been given its state, so the type system prevents us from serving it by accident before the state arrives. We attach the actual value later in exactly one place, and any handler expecting a different state type then fails to compile rather than failing at runtime, which is precisely the guarantee we want.

Serving with 'axum::serve'

The first edition started its server through **`axum::Server::bind`**, and that entry point no longer exists anywhere in the framework. Now that connection handling passes directly to Hyper, we create a Tokio listener ourselves and pass it to axum::serve with the router. That arrangement gives us direct control over the socket, which becomes useful later when we terminate TLS and again when we bind inside a container.

```
use tokio::net::TcpListener;


#[tokio::main]
async fn main() -> Result<(), Box<dyn std::error::Error>> {
    dotenvy::dotenv().ok();
    domain::telemetry::init_tracing(false);

    let state = AppState::new().await?;
    let app = build_router(state);

    let listener = TcpListener::bind("0.0.0.0:3000").await?;
    tracing::info!(addr = "0.0.0.0:3000", "LibroCommerce server
listening");
    axum::serve(listener, app).await?;

    Ok(())
}
```

In the above script, the **#[tokio::main]** attribute expands into a runtime that spawns one worker thread per available core and multiplexes every connection across them. Every handler therefore runs concurrently without us managing any threads at all, and a handler awaiting a slow database call yields its thread to other requests rather than blocking it. We tune that runtime deliberately later, though the defaults serve us well while we develop and carry most applications comfortably into production without adjustment.

We can now start the server and confirm that it binds correctly.

```
cargo run -p server-axum
```

The structured subscriber we built earlier formats the startup event, and the line below confirms the listener is accepting connections.

```
  2026-07-27T09:14:22.481Z  INFO server_axum: LibroCommerce
server listening

    at src/main.rs:18 addr="0.0.0.0:3000"
```

Typed Application State

Each handler needs access to the service implementations defined earlier, and Axum passes those through a state value that every handler can extract. We define that state as a single cloneable struct, where each service sits behind an **Arc** so that cloning the state costs a pointer copy rather than a deep duplication of everything inside it. The state also carries the Leptos configuration alongside the signing secret our authentication layer needs as shown below:

```
use std::sync::Arc;
use axum::extract::FromRef;
use leptos::config::LeptosOptions;

#[derive(Clone)]
pub struct AppState {
    pub leptos_options: LeptosOptions,
    pub inventory: Arc<InMemoryInventory>,
    pub orders: Arc<InMemoryOrders>,
    pub jwt_secret: Arc<String>,
}
```

```
impl FromRef<AppState> for LeptosOptions {
    fn from_ref(state: &AppState) -> Self {
        state.leptos_options.clone()
    }
}
```

Here, the **FromRef** implementation deserves a closer look, because Leptos requires it before it will accept our router. The Leptos routes expect **LeptosOptions** as their state, while our own handlers expect **AppState**, and **FromRef** teaches Axum how to derive the narrower type from the wider one. Both sets of routes therefore share a single state value without either of them knowing about the other, and adding a third consumer later needs only one further implementation.

These in-memory implementations stand in for the database we add later, and they satisfy exactly the traits declared earlier. So now, we will seed a handful of books so that the catalogue returns something meaningful while we develop.

```
use std::collections::HashMap;
use tokio::sync::RwLock;

pub struct InMemoryInventory {
    books: RwLock<HashMap<Uuid, Book>>,
}

impl InventoryService for InMemoryInventory {
    async fn find_book(&self, id: Uuid) -> Result<Book,
DomainError> {
        self.books
            .read()
            .await
            .get(&id)
            .cloned()
            .ok_or(DomainError::BookNotFound(id))
    }
```

```
    async fn list_books(&self, filter: BookFilter) ->
Result<Vec<Book>, DomainError> {
        let books = self.books.read().await;
        let matched = books
            .values()
            .filter(|b| !filter.in_stock_only || b.stock > 0)
            .filter(|b| filter.author.as_ref().is_none_or(|a|
&b.author == a))
            .skip(filter.offset as usize)
            .take(filter.limit.max(1) as usize)
            .cloned()
            .collect();
        Ok(matched)
    }

    async fn reserve_stock(&self, id: Uuid, quantity: i32) ->
Result<Book, DomainError> {
        let mut books = self.books.write().await;
        let book =
books.get_mut(&id).ok_or(DomainError::BookNotFound(id))?;
        if book.stock < quantity {
            return Err(DomainError::InsufficientStock { id,
available: book.stock });
        }
        book.stock -= quantity;
        Ok(book.clone())
    }
}
```

This implementation writes plain async fn rather than the explicit future syntax used in the trait declaration itself, and that difference is worth noticing. That shorthand is permitted inside an implementation because the compiler already knows the bound from the trait, so we gain the precision established earlier without repeating its verbosity in every method. The RwLock comes from Tokio rather than from the standard library, since a standard lock would block the entire runtime thread while it waits.

Mounting Leptos Application

The server delivers two quite different things, namely a JSON interface under /api and server-rendered views everywhere else. A router extension from Leptos registers every route it discovers from our component tree, so we never list those routes by hand and never forget one. We shall then compose both halves into a single router and attach the state that each of them draws upon. Both halves respond on the same port, so a visitor never notices the division at all.

```
use leptos_axum::{generate_route_list, LeptosRoutes};
use tower_http::trace::TraceLayer;

pub fn build_router(state: AppState) -> Router {
    let leptos_options = state.leptos_options.clone();
    let routes = generate_route_list(app::App);

    api_routes()
        .leptos_routes(&leptos_options, routes, {
            let options = leptos_options.clone();
            move || app::shell(options.clone())
        })
.fallback(leptos_axum::file_and_error_handler(app::shell))
        .layer(TraceLayer::new_for_http())
        .with_state(state)
}
```

The ordering inside that function carries real meaning rather than being arbitrary. Our API routes register first and therefore match before the Leptos catch-all considers a request, while the fallback serves static assets and renders our error view for anything unmatched. A layer added after both route sets wraps every one of them, which is exactly why the tracing layer sits where it does. The diagram below shows how a request travels through that arrangement.

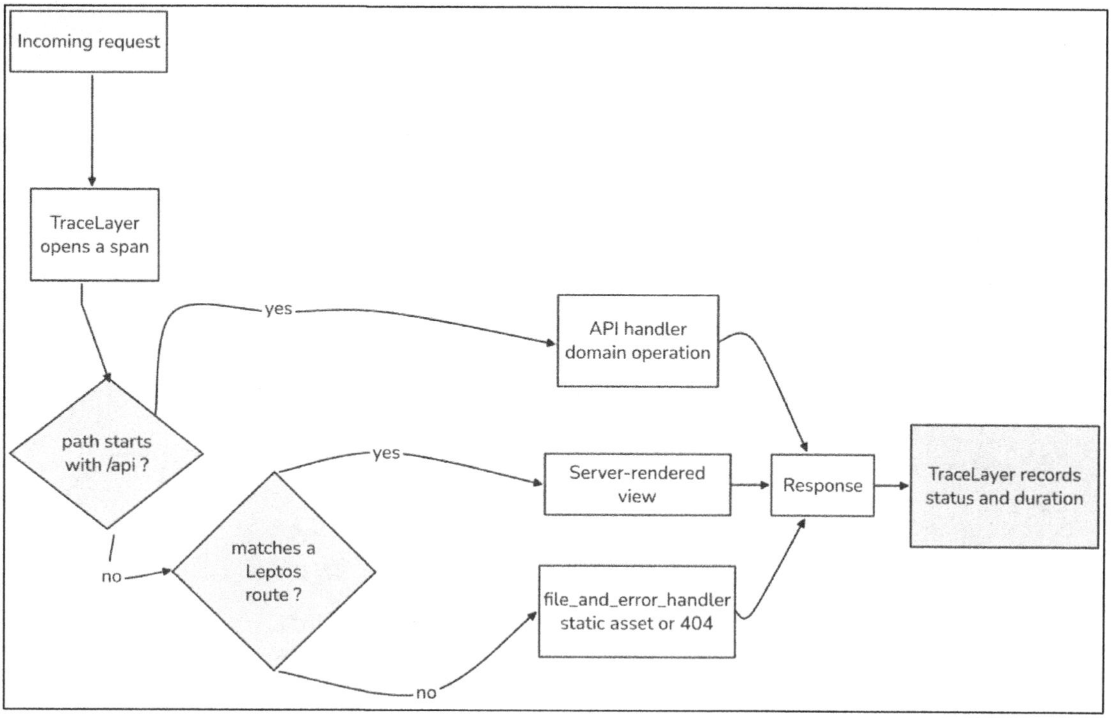

Translating Domain Operations into Handlers

Exposing Catalogue

We are now ready to write handlers, and each one stays deliberately thin throughout. These catalogue handlers extract what they need, call a domain method, and wrap the result, with no business logic appearing anywhere between those three steps. Each handler is built from its argument types alone, so a State extractor pulls our services, a Query extractor parses the query string, and a Path extractor supplies the identifier taken from the route. Not a line of manual parsing appears anywhere.

```
use axum::extract::{Path, Query, State};
use axum::Json;
use uuid::Uuid;

use domain::models::{Book, BookFilter};
use domain::services::InventoryService;
```

```
pub async fn list_books(
    State(state): State<AppState>,
    Query(filter): Query<BookFilter>,
) -> Result<Json<Vec<Book>>, ApiError> {
    let books = state.inventory.list_books(filter).await?;
    Ok(Json(books))
}

pub async fn find_book(
    State(state): State<AppState>,
    Path(id): Path<Uuid>,
) -> Result<Json<Book>, ApiError> {
    let book = state.inventory.find_book(id).await?;
    Ok(Json(book))
}
```

The Path<Uuid> extractor performs validation without any code from us, because a segment that fails to parse as a UUID never reaches the handler body at all. A 400 response goes back on our behalf, and our domain method therefore only ever receives values that are already well formed.

We can now exercise both routes against the running server.

```
curl -s
"http://localhost:3000/api/books?limit=2&in_stock_only=true"
```

The server responds with the seeded catalogue, serialized directly from our domain types.


```
[{"id":"6d0f...","isbn":"9781718503106","title":"Rust for
Rustaceans",
  "author":"Jon Gjengset","price_cents":4999,"stock":12,
  "published_on":"2021-12-21T00:00:00Z"}]
```


Placing and Tracking Orders

Rather more logic goes into order handling than into catalogue reading, though that logic belongs inside the domain rather than inside our handler. The endpoint accepts a JSON body, extracts the authenticated visitor from the request extensions that our middleware populates, and then delegates the actual work. We define a small request type so that clients never supply an order identifier or a status value of their own choosing. The server decides both of those instead, which closes an obvious avenue for tampering.

```
use axum::Extension;

use serde::Deserialize;


use domain::models::{Order, OrderLine, OrderStatus};

use domain::services::OrderService;


#[derive(Debug, Deserialize)]

pub struct PlaceOrderRequest {

    pub lines: Vec<OrderLine>,

}


pub async fn place_order(

    State(state): State<AppState>,

    Extension(claims): Extension<Claims>,

    Json(body): Json<PlaceOrderRequest>,

) -> Result<(StatusCode, Json<Order>), ApiError> {

    let order = state.orders.place_order(claims.sub,
body.lines).await?;

    Ok((StatusCode::CREATED, Json(order)))

}


pub async fn advance_status(

    State(state): State<AppState>,

    Path(id): Path<Uuid>,

    Json(next): Json<OrderStatus>,

) -> Result<Json<Order>, ApiError> {

    let order = state.orders.advance_status(id, next).await?;

    Ok(Json(order))
```

```
}
```

A pair of details inside place_order protects us from a common class of mistake. That identifier comes from the verified token rather than from the request body, so nobody can place an order against somebody else's account by editing a single JSON field. The return type also pairs a status code with the payload, which produces a 201 rather than the default 200, and that distinction matters to any client following HTTP conventions properly.

The order of arguments matters considerably more than it might first appear. An extractor that consumes the request body, such as Json, must sit last in the parameter list, because it takes ownership of the body while the others merely inspect the parts preceding it. That rule is enforced at compile time through two separate traits, and placing Json earlier produces an error mentioning FromRequestParts that reads confusingly until the underlying reason becomes familiar.

Mapping Domain Errors onto Status Codes

The domain methods return DomainError, while HTTP speaks in status codes, and exactly one place in the application should perform that translation. We define a wrapper type implementing Axum's response trait, and the **?** operator inside every handler then converts domain failures into it automatically. No handler therefore mentions a status code at all, which keeps each of them focused entirely on the operation it performs. A single change to the mapping then reaches every endpoint at once.

```
use axum::http::StatusCode;
use axum::response::{IntoResponse, Response};
use serde_json::json;

use domain::DomainError;

pub struct ApiError(pub DomainError);

impl From<DomainError> for ApiError {
    fn from(err: DomainError) -> Self {
        ApiError(err)
    }
}
```

```
impl IntoResponse for ApiError {
    fn into_response(self) -> Response {
        domain::telemetry::report(&self.0);

        let (status, message) = match &self.0 {
            DomainError::BookNotFound(_) |
DomainError::OrderNotFound(_) => {
                (StatusCode::NOT_FOUND, self.0.to_string())
            }
            DomainError::InsufficientStock { .. } => {
                (StatusCode::CONFLICT, self.0.to_string())
            }
            DomainError::InvalidTransition { .. } => {
                (StatusCode::UNPROCESSABLE_ENTITY,
self.0.to_string())
            }
            DomainError::InvalidCredentials => {
                (StatusCode::UNAUTHORIZED, "authentication
failed".to_owned())
            }
            DomainError::Storage(_) => {
                (StatusCode::INTERNAL_SERVER_ERROR, "internal
error".to_owned())
            }
        };

        (status, Json(json!({ "error": message
}))).into_response()
    }
}
```

A single decision inside that match concerns security rather than correctness. The storage variant returns a generic phrase rather than the underlying message, because a database failure frequently contains table names, column names, or fragments of a query, and none of that belongs in a response sent to an unknown client. We still record the full cause through the reporting function built earlier, so our logs keep everything an engineer needs while our responses reveal nothing useful to an attacker.

The remaining variants return their own messages deliberately, since each one describes a condition the client caused and can therefore correct without our help. A visitor told that only three copies remain can adjust the quantity and retry immediately, whereas a visitor told merely that something failed can do nothing at all. Throughout the whole application, we distinguish failures the caller can act upon from failures that belong solely to us.

Integrating Third-party APIs

Fetching Metadata from OpenLibrary

That catalogue holds titles and authors, though visitors expect cover images and descriptions that we would rather not maintain ourselves. The OpenLibrary service publishes that data freely against an ISBN, so we fetch it at request time and enrich our own records with it. That client lives inside the server crate rather than the domain crate, because an outbound HTTP call is an infrastructure concern and our domain layer must stay entirely free of such things.

```
use std::time::Duration;
use reqwest::Client;
use serde::Deserialize;

#[derive(Debug, Clone, Deserialize)]
pub struct CoverMetadata {
    #[serde(default)]
    pub description: Option<String>,
    #[serde(default)]
    pub number_of_pages: Option<u32>,
}

pub struct OpenLibraryClient {
    http: Client,
}
```

```
impl OpenLibraryClient {
    pub fn new() -> Self {
        let http = Client::builder()
            .timeout(Duration::from_secs(3))
            .user_agent("LibroCommerce/0.1")
            .build()
            .expect("failed to build HTTP client");
        Self { http }
    }

    pub async fn lookup(&self, isbn: &str) ->
Option<CoverMetadata> {
        let url =
format!("https://openlibrary.org/isbn/{isbn}.json");
        match self.http.get(&url).send().await {
            Ok(resp) if resp.status().is_success() =>
resp.json().await.ok(),
            Ok(resp) => {
                tracing::warn!(status = %resp.status(), isbn,
"metadata lookup rejected");
                None
            }
            Err(err) => {
                tracing::warn!(error = %err, isbn, "metadata
lookup failed");
                None
            }
        }
    }
}
```

The client builds once and lives inside the application state, because a reqwest::Client owns a connection pool and constructing a new one per request discards that pool entirely. A single reused client keeps connections alive between calls, which removes a full TLS handshake from most lookups and noticeably reduces latency. We also set an explicit user agent, since many public interfaces throttle or reject outright any request that fails to identify itself properly. That agent string names both the application and its version.

Handling Timeouts and Failures

The return type of our lookup method encodes a deliberate policy, because it produces an **`Option`** rather than a **`Result`**. Missing cover metadata is a cosmetic shortfall rather than a failure of the request itself, so a slow or unavailable third party must never prevent a visitor from viewing a book. The handler therefore treats missing metadata as an ordinary outcome and renders the view regardless, while the warning we logged preserves every detail for later investigation.

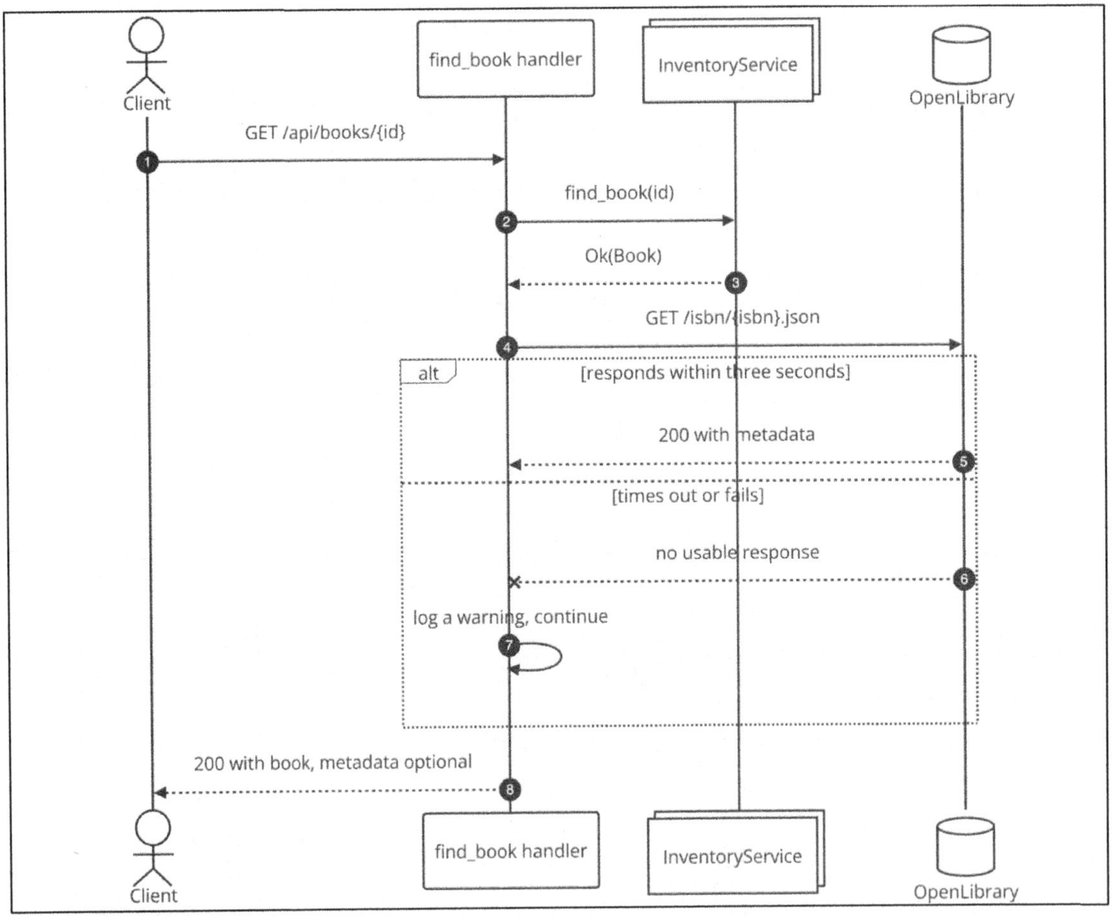

The three-second timeout sits on the client rather than on individual calls, so every request inherits it without us remembering to apply one each time. An outbound call lacking a timeout will eventually hang for as long as the operating system permits, and a handful of such calls can exhaust the connection pool while the runtime simply waits. We revisit this ground later when we add backpressure, though a timeout on every outbound client remains the single most valuable safeguard available.

Securing and Logging Requests

Issuing JSON Web Tokens

All authentication rests on signed tokens, and we pinned jsonwebtoken at version 10 with the rust_crypto backend earlier for reasons worth restating here. That release requires an explicit choice of cryptographic backend, and the pure Rust option avoids any dependency on a system C compiler, which keeps our build self-contained. A published security advisory hangs over version 9, so remaining on the older release was never a genuine option for us. That pinned choice therefore reflects security rather than preference.

```
use chrono::{Duration, Utc};
use jsonwebtoken::{encode, EncodingKey, Header};
use serde::{Deserialize, Serialize};

#[derive(Debug, Clone, Serialize, Deserialize)]
pub struct Claims {
    pub sub: Uuid,
    pub email: String,
    pub exp: i64,
    pub iat: i64,
}

pub fn issue_token(user: &User, secret: &str) -> Result<String, DomainError> {
    let now = Utc::now();
    let claims = Claims {
        sub: user.id,
        email: user.email.clone(),
        iat: now.timestamp(),
        exp: (now + Duration::hours(12)).timestamp(),
    };
```

```
    encode(&Header::default(), &claims,
&EncodingKey::from_secret(secret.as_bytes()))
        .map_err(|e| DomainError::Storage(Box::new(e)))
}
```

The claims carry only what every request genuinely needs, namely the visitor identifier and their email address. A token travels with every single request and appears in proxy logs and in browser storage, so placing a display name, a role list, or anything sensitive inside it costs us privacy while saving very little indeed. The twelve-hour expiry balances convenience against exposure, and we add refresh handling later, once our sessions live in Redis. A shorter lifetime would frustrate visitors without meaningfully improving safety.

Verifying Tokens in Middleware

We protect routes through middleware rather than through checks inside each handler, so that a new endpoint cannot accidentally ship without protection attached to it. Middleware in Axum is built from an ordinary asynchronous function, where we inspect the request, decide whether it may proceed, and then either call the next layer or return early. This function also inserts the verified claims into the request extensions, which is how place_order received them earlier. That protection therefore attaches to the router rather than to our discipline.

```
use axum::extract::Request;
use axum::http::header;
use axum::middleware::Next;
use jsonwebtoken::{decode, DecodingKey, Validation};

pub async fn require_auth(
    State(state): State<AppState>,
    mut request: Request,
    next: Next,
) -> Result<Response, ApiError> {
    let token = request
        .headers()
        .get(header::AUTHORIZATION)
        .and_then(|value| value.to_str().ok())
        .and_then(|value| value.strip_prefix("Bearer "))
```

```
        .ok_or(DomainError::InvalidCredentials)?;

    let data = decode::<Claims>(
        token,
        &DecodingKey::from_secret(state.jwt_secret.as_bytes()),
        &Validation::default(),
    )
    .map_err(|_| DomainError::InvalidCredentials)?;

    request.extensions_mut().insert(data.claims);
    Ok(next.run(request).await)
}
```

We attach that function to the routes needing protection, and our choice of method matters quite a lot. A **route_layer** applies only to routes already registered on the router, whereas a plain **layer** would also wrap the fallback and reject requests for missing paths with a 401 rather than a 404. Meanwhile the login endpoint stays outside the protected group entirely, since a visitor cannot present a token before receiving one. The public and protected groups therefore stay clearly separated.

```
use axum::middleware;

pub fn api_routes(state: AppState) -> Router<AppState> {
    let protected = Router::new()
        .route("/api/orders", post(place_order))
        .route("/api/orders/{id}", get(find_order))
        .route("/api/orders/{id}/status", post(advance_status))
        .route_layer(middleware::from_fn_with_state(state,
require_auth));

    Router::new()
        .route("/api/books", get(list_books))
        .route("/api/books/{id}", get(find_book))
        .route("/api/auth/login", post(login))
```

```
            .merge(protected)
}
```

The **`Validation::default()`** value already checks expiry on our behalf, so a stale token fails verification without any explicit comparison written by us. We could tighten that validation further by requiring an issuer or an audience claim, and applications serving several clients from one signing key generally should do exactly that. A single frontend needs neither of those, though the option stays available whenever our situation changes later.

Layering Tracing over Router

This tracing layer wraps every route, and it produces one span per request that nests around everything the handler subsequently does. The instrumented service methods built earlier therefore appear inside that request span automatically, and following a single request through several layers needs no correlation identifier threaded through our signatures by hand. We refine the default configuration so that our spans carry precisely the fields we search on later. The field names we choose now determine which queries stay possible in production.

```
use tower_http::trace::{DefaultOnResponse, TraceLayer};

use tracing::Level;


pub fn trace_layer() -> TraceLayer<


tower_http::classify::SharedClassifier<tower_http::classify::Serv
erErrorsAsFailures>,

> {

    TraceLayer::new_for_http()

        .make_span_with(|request: &Request| {

            tracing::info_span!(

                "http",

                method = %request.method(),

                uri = %request.uri().path(),

                status = tracing::field::Empty,

            )

        })

        .on_response(DefaultOnResponse::new().level(Level::INFO))
```

}

The span records the path rather than the full URI quite deliberately, because a query string may carry a search term, an email address, or a token supplied by mistake. A path-only record keeps our logs useful while avoiding any accidental capture of visitor data, which matters both for privacy and for the retention policies most organizations operate under. The diagram below traces an authenticated request through every layer we have now assembled.

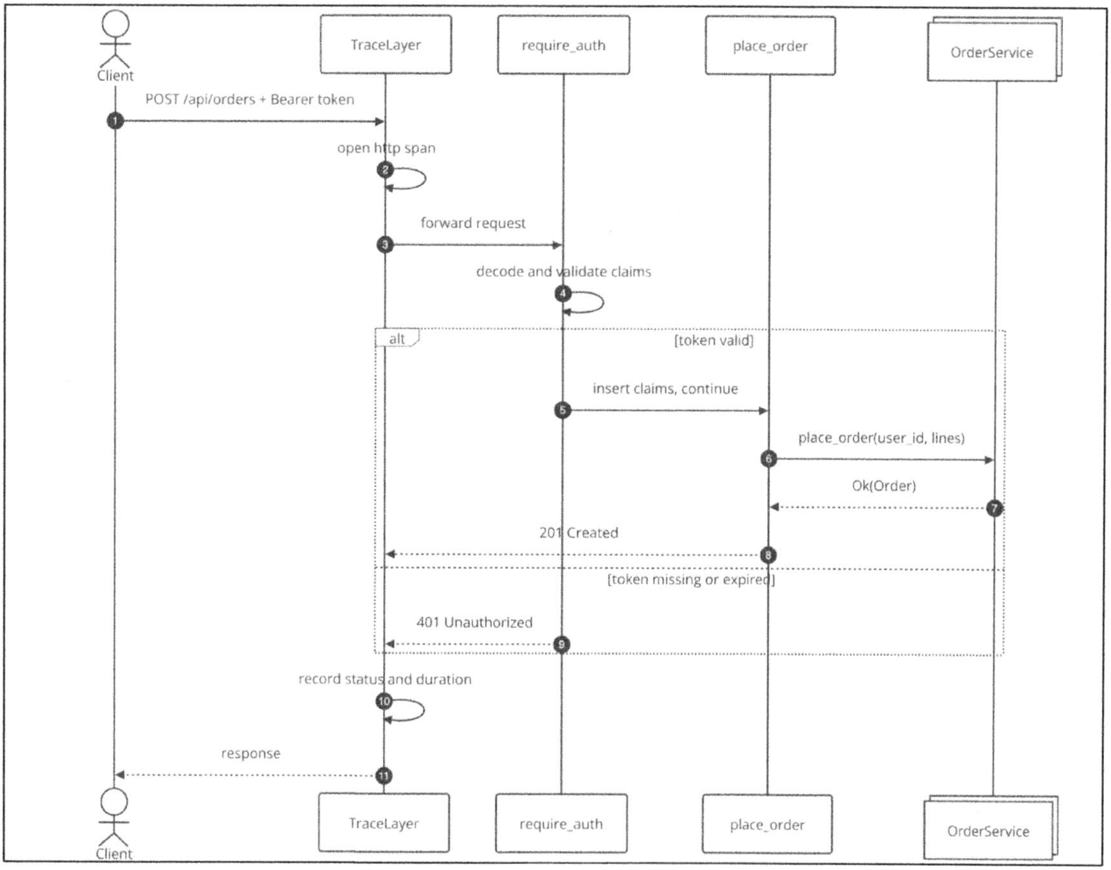

We can now verify the whole arrangement by requesting a protected route without credentials.

```
curl -s -o /dev/null -w "%{http_code}\n" -X POST
http://localhost:3000/api/orders
```

The server rejects the request before any handler runs, and our span records the outcome alongside the timing.

```
401
  2026-07-27T09:22:07.114Z  INFO http{method=POST
uri=/api/orders}:
```

```
finished processing request latency=0 ms status=401
```

Summary

We fitted a complete web layer around the architecture from Chapter 2 without placing a single business rule anywhere inside it. Our routes adopt the brace syntax that Axum 0.8 introduced, our server starts through **`axum::serve`** with a listener we own outright, and our application state carries both the domain services and the Leptos configuration behind one **`FromRef`** implementation. We also mounted the JSON interface and the server-rendered views onto a single router with a deliberate ordering.

We then wrote handlers that extract, delegate, and wrap, and we translated every domain failure into a status code in exactly one place while keeping storage details well away from client responses. Our OpenLibrary client demonstrated a timeout-bounded outbound call whose failure degrades gracefully, and our middleware now verifies signed tokens before any protected route executes. In Chapter 4, we rebuild this entire layer on Actix Web, reusing the domain crate and changing nothing beneath it. That exercise proves the architecture rather than merely describing it.

CHAPTER 4
BUILDING SERVER WITH ACTIX WEB

We will now rebuild that same web layer on Actix Web, and the exercise tests whether our architecture genuinely holds together under substitution. Our **domain** crate stays untouched, our service traits stay untouched, and our in-memory implementations stay untouched, so the only code we write concerns translating HTTP into domain calls a second time. Whatever we find ourselves unable to reuse would signal a leak in the boundary we drew. So far, nothing suggests one exists.

We are going to concentrate on what makes Actix Web different rather than on what the two frameworks share between them. Attention falls first on its threading model, which runs an independent runtime per worker, and thereby frees our handlers from the Send requirement, along with its routing primitives, its ResponseError trait, and its middleware traits. By the close of this chapter, one binary will serve LibroCommerce through Axum and a second through Actix Web.

Understanding Actix Web Runtime

Workers, Arbiters and Per-thread Runtimes

The way Actix Web organizes concurrency differs quite sharply from the runtime underneath Axum, and that difference explains nearly every other distinction between the two frameworks. Tokio's standard scheduler runs one multi-threaded work-stealing pool, where any task may migrate from the thread that spawned it to whichever thread falls idle first. Instead, several independent single-threaded runtimes start under Actix Web, each one called an arbiter, with one pinned to every worker thread. A connection accepted by a given worker then stays on that worker for its entire life.

Each arbiter owns a complete copy of our application, listens on the shared socket, and drives its own futures to completion without ever handing one to a sibling. Work spreads across workers because the operating system distributes incoming connections between them, not because tasks move around after the fact. That arrangement trades a little scheduling fairness for a considerable simplification, since no future ever crosses a thread boundary once it has begun executing on a particular arbiter.

The consequence reaches directly into the code we write every day. A future that never migrates needs no proof that it is safe to migrate, so Actix Web imposes no **Send** bound on handler return types at all. The traits we declared earlier carry that bound anyway because Axum requires it, and Actix Web accepts the stricter guarantee without complaint. Code written exclusively for Actix Web could drop the bound entirely and use single-threaded types such as Rc inside a handler body.

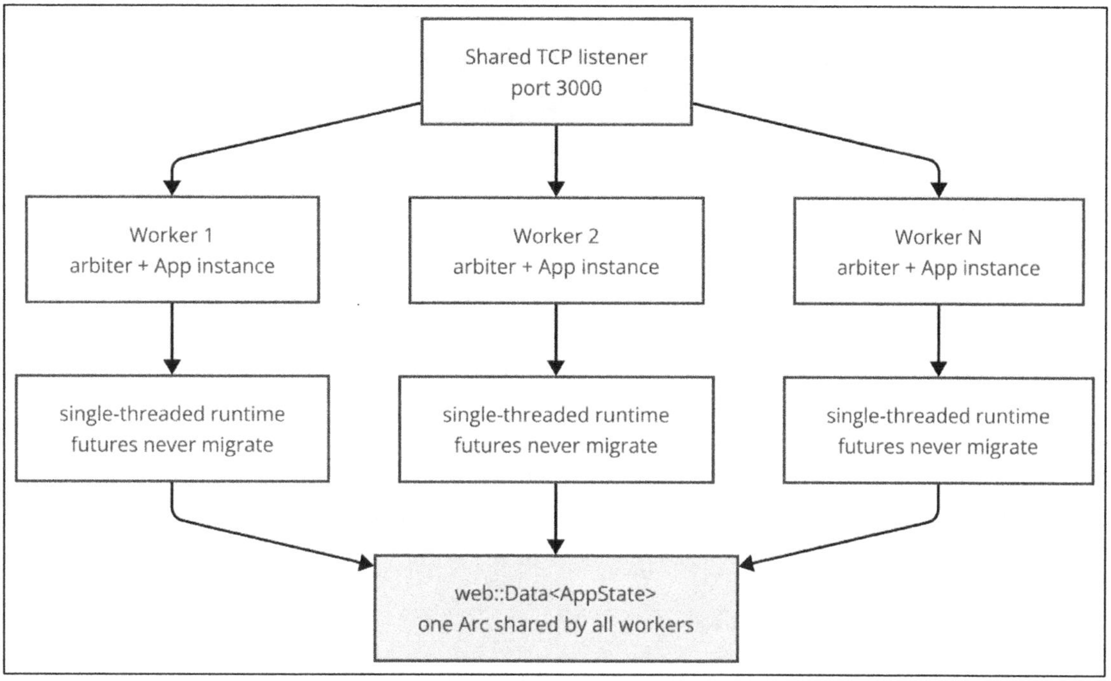

Why Handlers Need No Send Bound?

The practical gain from that model appears whenever a type resists sharing between threads. Plenty of parsers, template engines, and client libraries hold internal buffers that make them **!Send**, and a handler on Axum must either wrap such a value in a mutex or construct a fresh one for every request. Each option costs us something, since a mutex serializes access across every worker while repeated construction discards whatever setup the value performed on creation. Both costs recur on every single request.

Under Actix Web, we may hold one instance per worker instead, with no lock and no repeated construction anywhere. We register that value through **App::app_data** inside the factory closure rather than outside it, which produces exactly one copy per arbiter. Each worker then reads its own copy without any contention, and the total memory cost equals the worker quantity multiplied by a single instance, which usually amounts to a trivial figure on modern hardware.

```
use std::cell::RefCell;

use actix_web::{web, App, HttpServer};


struct PerWorkerCache {

    recent: RefCell<Vec<Uuid>>,

}
```

```
HttpServer::new(move || {
    App::new()
        .app_data(web::Data::new(shared_state.clone()))
        .app_data(PerWorkerCache { recent:
RefCell::new(Vec::new()) })
})
```

A pair of registrations appears in that closure, and the two behave in opposite ways from one another. The first clones an **Arc** created beforehand, so every worker points at exactly one shared value. Its counterpart constructs a new PerWorkerCache on each invocation, so every worker receives its own instance holding a RefCell that would never compile on Axum. That choice depends entirely on whether the data must stay consistent across workers or may safely diverge.

Sharing State with 'web::Data'

The application factory runs once per worker rather than once per process, and that single fact produces the most common defect in Actix Web applications. State constructed inside the closure multiplies silently, so a connection pool created there opens one pool per worker while a counter created there tallies only the requests handled by its own thread. The compiler flags neither mistake, and both surface later as puzzling inconsistencies under load.

We therefore build shared state before the factory and clone a handle into it, which is precisely what the code below demonstrates. The **web::Data** wrapper holds an Arc internally, so each clone costs an atomic increment rather than a duplication of the underlying value.

```
use actix_web::{middleware::Logger, web, App, HttpServer};


#[actix_web::main]
async fn main() -> std::io::Result<()> {
    dotenvy::dotenv().ok();
    domain::telemetry::init_tracing(false);


    let state = web::Data::new(AppState::new().await);


    HttpServer::new(move || {
        App::new()
```

```
            .app_data(state.clone())
            .wrap(Logger::default())
            .configure(register_api)
    })
    .bind(("0.0.0.0", 3000))?
    .run()
    .await
}
```

This **#[actix_web::main]** attribute differs from the Tokio equivalent, because it starts an Actix System that supervises the arbiters rather than a plain work-stealing runtime. The **bind** call binds the listener before any worker starts, so a port conflict fails at startup rather than deep inside a worker thread. By default, the worker count matches the available parallelism of the machine, and **HttpServer::workers** overrides that default whenever we need a fixed number instead. Inside a container we often set it explicitly.

Each handler reaches the shared value through an extractor, and our catalogue handlers below show the resulting shape. Every one of them mirrors its earlier counterpart while using the Actix extractor family instead.

```
use actix_web::web;
use domain::services::InventoryService;


pub async fn list_books(
    state: web::Data<AppState>,
    filter: web::Query<BookFilter>,
) -> Result<web::Json<Vec<Book>>, ApiError> {
    let books =
state.inventory.list_books(filter.into_inner()).await?;
    Ok(web::Json(books))
}


pub async fn find_book(
    state: web::Data<AppState>,
    path: web::Path<Uuid>,
```

```
) -> Result<web::Json<Book>, ApiError> {
    let book =
state.inventory.find_book(path.into_inner()).await?;
    Ok(web::Json(book))
}
```

A constraint that shaped our Axum handlers disappears here entirely and without ceremony. Every argument resolves through a single FromRequest trait rather than through separate body and non-body extraction traits, so a web::Json argument may sit in any position within the parameter list. As many as twelve extractors combine in any order at all, and the compiler never objects to an arrangement that Axum would reject outright. Each signature therefore reads in whatever order suits it best.

Composing Routes with Scopes and Guards

Scopes, Resources and Named Routes

Routing in Actix Web is built from three nested concepts rather than from one flat table of paths. A scope owns a path prefix and may carry its own middleware, a resource owns a specific path pattern and may carry several methods, and a route binds one method to one handler. One scope nested inside another composes both prefixes, so our protected order endpoints inherit the /api prefix and any middleware attached above them without restating either one.

```
use actix_web::web::{self, ServiceConfig};


pub fn register_api(cfg: &mut ServiceConfig) {
    cfg.service(
        web::scope("/api")
            .service(
                web::resource("/books")
                    .name("book_list")
                    .route(web::get().to(list_books)),
            )
            .service(
                web::resource("/books/{id}")
                    .name("book_detail")
```

```
                    .route(web::get().to(find_book)),
            )
.service(web::resource("/auth/login").route(web::post().to(login)
)),
    );
}
```

The **name** calls introduce a facility with no Axum counterpart at all, namely reverse URL generation. A handler or a template may ask the request to build a URL for a named resource, supplying the dynamic segments, and Actix Web then assembles the path from the pattern it already holds. Every link therefore stays correct whenever a path changes, because exactly one definition exists and every reference derives from it rather than repeating it. A broken link therefore becomes a compile-time concern.

```
use actix_web::HttpRequest;

pub fn detail_link(req: &HttpRequest, id: Uuid) -> String {
    req.url_for("book_detail", [id.to_string()])
        .map(|url| url.to_string())
        .unwrap_or_else(|_| format!("/api/books/{id}"))
}
```

The ServiceConfig parameter also deserves attention, because it solves a problem the factory closure creates for us. We must register routes inside that closure, so the work repeats on every worker, which makes a long inline chain awkward to read and impossible to reuse elsewhere. A configuration function accepts the mutable config, registers everything, and stays testable on its own, so our factory shrinks to a single **configure** call regardless of how many endpoints we add.

Filtering Requests with Guards

A guard lets a resource decline a request before any handler runs at all, and it may inspect anything present in the request head. The framework supplies guards for methods, headers, hosts, and query parameters, then combines them through guard::Any and guard::All. A pair of resources may therefore share one path while serving entirely different clients, with the guard deciding which of them responds to any given request. This routing table therefore carries decisions that would otherwise sit inside handler bodies.

```
use actix_web::guard;
```

```
web::scope("/api")
    .service(
        web::resource("/books")
            .guard(guard::Header("accept", "application/json"))
            .route(web::get().to(list_books)),
    )
    .service(
        web::resource("/books")
            .route(web::get().to(render_book_list_html)),
    )
```

Both resources above register the identical path, and Actix Web tries each in turn until a guard admits the request. A client asking for JSON reaches our API handler, while a browser asking for HTML falls through to the second resource instead. Negotiation over content therefore lives inside the routing table rather than inside a handler that inspects headers and branches, which keeps every handler focused on producing exactly one representation. Not one of the handlers inspects a header at all.

Versioning and staged rollouts also express themselves cleanly through guards, since a custom guard is any type implementing one single method. A guard matching a header such as **`x-api-version: 2`** routes newer clients to a newer handler while older clients continue reaching the original, and both versions coexist under one path until the migration finishes. On Axum, similar outcomes come from nested routers and manual header inspection, though the intent reads considerably less clearly there. The routing therefore stays declarative on Actix Web.

Mounting Leptos on Actix

The Leptos integration changes crate but not shape, since leptos_actix mirrors the Axum companion closely throughout. We register the generated route list, supply the same shell function, and serve the WebAssembly bundle through the static file service that Actix Web provides as a separate crate. This workspace manifest gains three entries before any of that compiles successfully.

```
[workspace.dependencies]
actix-web = "4.13.0"
actix-files = "0.6"
leptos_actix = "0.8.19"
```

Once those resolve, we extend the feature set established earlier so that the app crate can compile against either integration. That second backend feature sits alongside the first rather than replacing it.

```
[features]
default = []
hydrate = ["leptos/hydrate"]
ssr = ["leptos/ssr", "dep:domain"]
backend-axum = ["ssr", "dep:leptos_axum"]
backend-actix = ["ssr", "dep:leptos_actix"]
```

That factory then composes the API scope, the Leptos routes, and the asset service into one application. The order of registration matters as it did before, though Actix Web resolves matches by first registered rather than by specificity.

```
use actix_files::Files;
use leptos_actix::{generate_route_list, LeptosRoutes};

HttpServer::new(move || {
    let routes = generate_route_list(app::App);
    let options = leptos_options.clone();

    App::new()
        .app_data(state.clone())
        .app_data(web::Data::new(options.clone()))
        .wrap(Logger::default())
        .configure(register_api)
        .service(Files::new("/pkg", format!("{}/pkg",
options.site_root)))
        .leptos_routes(routes, {
            let options = options.clone();
            move || app::shell(options.clone())
        })
})
```

The **generate_route_list** call sits inside the closure rather than outside it, which looks wasteful and genuinely is not. That call renders our component tree once to discover its routes, and each worker needs its own list because the resulting structures never get shared between arbiters. The shell closure clones the options again for exactly the same reason, since every arbiter builds its own service tree independently during startup.

Reporting Failures with ResponseError

Implementing ResponseError for DomainError

Error conversion here runs through a dedicated trait rather than through a response conversion, and the difference goes deeper than cosmetics. Our type implements **ResponseError**, which requires **Display** and **Debug** alongside two methods, and any handler returning **Result<T, ApiError>** then compiles without further ceremony. The trait separates the status code from the body, so middleware and error handlers may consult the status without constructing a full response first. That split proves useful more often than it first appears.

```
use std::fmt;
use actix_web::{http::StatusCode, HttpResponse, ResponseError};
use serde_json::json;

use domain::DomainError;

#[derive(Debug)]
pub struct ApiError(pub DomainError);

impl From<DomainError> for ApiError {
    fn from(err: DomainError) -> Self {
        ApiError(err)
    }
}

impl fmt::Display for ApiError {
    fn fmt(&self, f: &mut fmt::Formatter<'_>) -> fmt::Result {
```

```
            write!(f, "{}", self.0)
        }
    }

    impl ResponseError for ApiError {
        fn status_code(&self) -> StatusCode {
            match &self.0 {
                DomainError::BookNotFound(_) |
    DomainError::OrderNotFound(_) => StatusCode::NOT_FOUND,
                DomainError::InsufficientStock { .. } =>
    StatusCode::CONFLICT,
                DomainError::InvalidTransition { .. } =>
    StatusCode::UNPROCESSABLE_ENTITY,
                DomainError::InvalidCredentials =>
    StatusCode::UNAUTHORIZED,
                DomainError::Storage(_) =>
    StatusCode::INTERNAL_SERVER_ERROR,
            }
        }

        fn error_response(&self) -> HttpResponse {
            domain::telemetry::report(&self.0);

            let message = match &self.0 {
                DomainError::Storage(_) => "internal
    error".to_owned(),
                DomainError::InvalidCredentials => "authentication
    failed".to_owned(),
                other => other.to_string(),
            };

            HttpResponse::build(self.status_code()).json(json!({
    "error": message }))
        }
```

```
}
```

Our implementation reaches the identical outcome as before while splitting the decision across two separate methods. The status mapping now lives alone inside **`status_code`**, which any caller may query without building a response at all, and the body construction lives alone inside **`error_response`**. A default implementation of **`error_response`** already produces a plain response from the status and the **`Display`** output, so overriding it stays optional whenever a JSON body is not required.

Comparing Two Error Mechanisms

The two designs diverge most visibly around composition rather than around correctness. On Axum, a wrapper type becomes necessary whenever a foreign error must become a response, because the orphan rule forbids implementing IntoResponse for a type declared elsewhere. The identical restriction applies on Actix Web, though its ecosystem softens the impact because many crates implement ResponseError themselves, so an error from a compatible library often converts without any wrapper written by us. Our own wrapper stays necessary regardless.

The automatic conversion also behaves differently in everyday practice. A universal actix_web::Error absorbs anything implementing ResponseError, and a handler may return that type to mix several error families within one signature. Our single **`DomainError`** makes the facility unnecessary here, though applications aggregating failures from many libraries frequently return the universal type and let each library supply its own status mapping. Those applications gain considerably from the arrangement, while ours would gain very little indeed.

A decisive advantage belongs to neither approach, and both keep the mapping in exactly one place. The Actix Web trait suits applications assembling many third-party errors, since much of the mapping arrives already written by somebody else. Its Axum counterpart suits applications defining their own error surface deliberately, since one implementation covers everything and nothing converts by surprise. Our architecture already produces a single error type, so we gain equally little from either convenience.

Protecting Routes with Actix Middleware

Writing Middleware with 'from_fn'

Middleware here is built from the framework's own service traits rather than from tower, and the modern shorthand accepts an ordinary asynchronous function. Our function receives the request alongside a handle to the remainder of the chain, inspects whatever it needs, and then either continues or returns early. Values travel forward to handlers through extensions on the request, exactly as they did on the previous backend, so nothing downstream changes. Every handler remains entirely unaware of the layer above it.

```
use actix_web::body::MessageBody;
use actix_web::dev::{ServiceRequest, ServiceResponse};
use actix_web::middleware::Next;
use actix_web::{http::header, web, Error, HttpMessage};
use jsonwebtoken::{decode, DecodingKey, Validation};

pub async fn require_auth(
    req: ServiceRequest,
    next: Next<impl MessageBody + 'static>,
) -> Result<ServiceResponse<impl MessageBody>, Error> {
    let secret = req
        .app_data::<web::Data<AppState>>()
        .map(|state| state.jwt_secret.clone())
        .ok_or_else(||
ApiError::from(DomainError::InvalidCredentials))?;

    let token = req
        .headers()
        .get(header::AUTHORIZATION)
        .and_then(|value| value.to_str().ok())
        .and_then(|value| value.strip_prefix("Bearer "))
        .ok_or_else(||
ApiError::from(DomainError::InvalidCredentials))?
        .to_owned();

    let data = decode::<Claims>(
        &token,
        &DecodingKey::from_secret(secret.as_bytes()),
        &Validation::default(),
    )
    .map_err(|_|
ApiError::from(DomainError::InvalidCredentials))?;
```

```
    req.extensions_mut().insert(data.claims);
    next.call(req).await
}
```

This function reaches application state through req.app_data rather than through an extractor, since middleware runs before extraction has begun. That lookup returns an **Option**, because middleware may in principle run on an application where the value was never registered at all, and our fallback treats any absence as an authentication failure. We then attach the middleware to a scope, which protects everything nested inside it however deeply. A single wrap therefore covers an entire branch of the routing tree.

```
use actix_web::middleware::from_fn;


web::scope("/orders")
    .wrap(from_fn(require_auth))

.service(web::resource("").route(web::post().to(place_order)))

.service(web::resource("/{id}").route(web::get().to(find_order)))

.service(web::resource("/{id}/status").route(web::post().to(advan
ce_status)))
```

A wrap at scope level avoids the distinction that governed our earlier backend, because a scope covers only the resources registered within it and never the surrounding application. Any path outside the scope that matches nothing reaches the default handler untouched, so a request for a nonexistent route still produces the response it properly should. The protected group therefore stays visually obvious inside the routing code, which makes an unprotected addition considerably harder to overlook during review. A reviewer therefore sees the boundary directly.

Building Stateful Middleware with Transform

The shorthand suits stateless checks well, though middleware holding configuration or long-lived resources needs the underlying trait pair instead. Actix Web splits that work between Transform, which builds the middleware once per worker during startup, and Service, which handles each request afterwards. That separation lets expensive setup happen exactly once while the per-request path stays as lean as possible. The rate limiter below illustrates the arrangement, since it holds both a configured limit and a running tally.

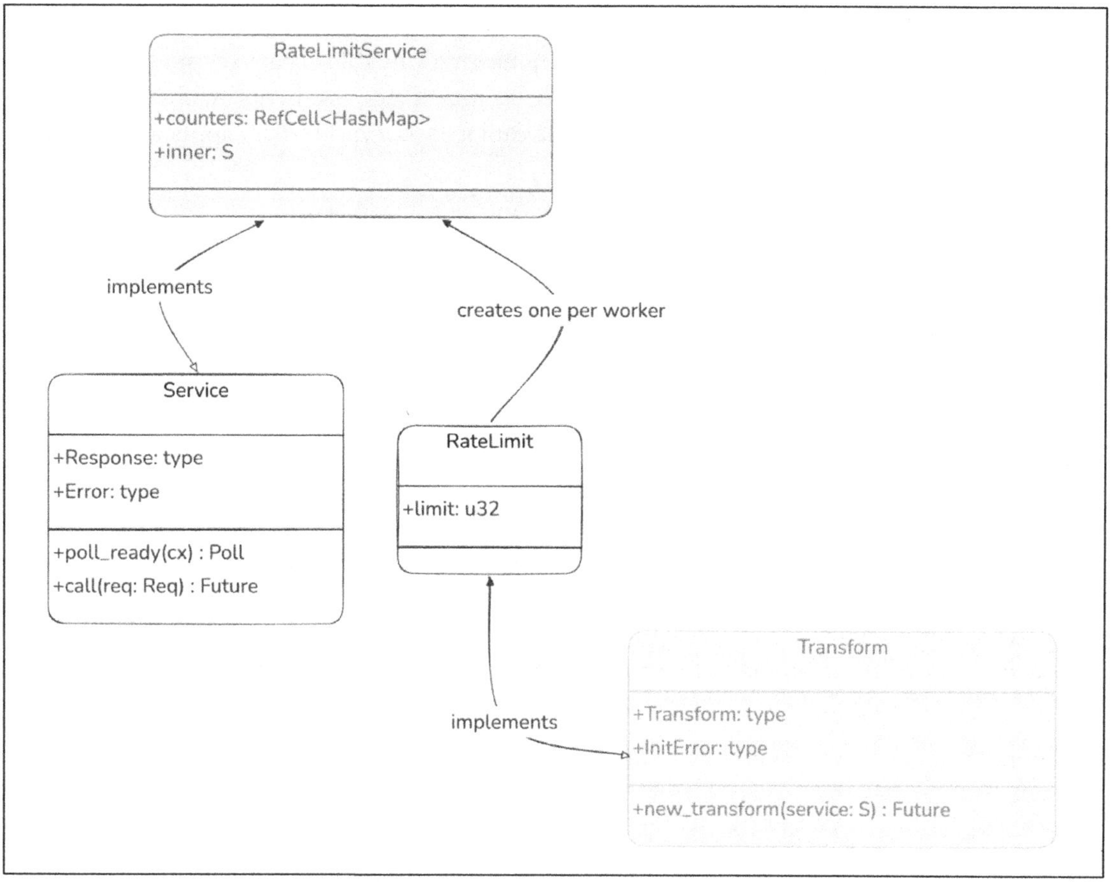

The lifecycle reads clearly from that relationship. Our **`RateLimit`** value carries configuration and lives inside the factory closure, **`new_transform`** runs once per worker and produces a **`RateLimitService`** wrapping the next service in the chain, and **`call`** then runs for every request. A tally held inside the service needs no lock at all, because each worker owns its own instance and the arbiter never shares it, which returns us to the threading model from the opening section.

The framework also ships a useful middleware collection that saves us writing several of these ourselves. **`Among them, Compress negotiates response encoding, NormalizePath resolves trailing slash mismatches before routing, DefaultHeaders applies security headers to every response, and Logger records access lines.`** We configure the security headers and compression deliberately for production later, so we leave every default in place for the moment and move on. Each one costs a single **`wrap`** call and carries no additional dependency into our build.

Choosing between Two Backends

We now hold two working backends, and an honest comparison serves us better than any preference would. The lead on routing expressiveness belongs to Actix Web through guards and named resources, on extractor flexibility through unrestricted argument ordering, and on freedom from the Send bound, which matters whenever a valuable library resists sharing across threads. Its bundled middleware also covers common requirements without additional dependencies or configuration work. Those advantages compound in applications serving several client families at once.

The lead for Axum comes from its position inside the tower ecosystem, where any tower middleware written for any tower service works unchanged. That reach brings timeouts, retries, load shedding, concurrency limits, and rate limiting from crates that never mention Axum at all, and the identical layers apply to a gRPC service built on tonic. A smaller dependency graph also comes out of Axum, and its state handling stays uniform because the work-stealing runtime removes any per-worker distinction. That state handling stayed simpler there as a result.

Our recommendation follows the surrounding system rather than the frameworks themselves. A service sitting alongside gRPC components or reusing tower layers fits Axum naturally and needs little argument. One needing content negotiation, reverse URL generation, or a !Send dependency fits Actix Web instead. Our application runs comfortably on either, which is exactly what our architecture was designed to demonstrate from the beginning. Whichever we choose, nothing we need later becomes unavailable, since the domain crate stays identical either way.

We can now run the Actix Web binary and confirm it behaves identically.

```
cargo run -p server-actix --features backend-actix
```

The server reports its worker configuration and begins accepting connections on the same port our earlier binary used.

```
  2026-07-27T10:41:03.226Z  INFO actix_server::builder: starting
8 workers
  2026-07-27T10:41:03.227Z  INFO actix_server::server: Actix
runtime found; starting in
    Actix runtime, workers: 8, listening on: 0.0.0.0:3000
```

Summary

We rebuilt the entire web layer on Actix Web without altering a single line inside the domain crate, which validates the boundary drawn in Chapter 2 more convincingly than any argument could manage. Our attention stayed on the framework's threading model, where an arbiter per worker runs a single-threaded runtime and no future ever migrates between threads. That model removes the **Send** requirement from handlers and permits one unshared instance of an awkward dependency per worker.

We then met the routing primitives that distinguish Actix Web, namely scopes carrying their own middleware, resources supporting reverse URL generation, and guards deciding admission before any handler runs. Our error type reached the same outcome through **`ResponseError`**, splitting status selection from body construction, and our authentication moved into a scope-wrapped function. In Chapter 5, we now replace our in-memory implementations with PostgreSQL, and neither backend will require any change at all. That claim is the strongest test our architecture faces.

CHAPTER 5

DATABASE INTEGRATION AND STATE MANAGEMENT

We will now replace the in-memory implementations that carried Chapter 3 and 4 with PostgreSQL, and both backends must accept that replacement without a single alteration to either one. These service traits already describe every operation the storage layer performs, so the work ahead consists of satisfying those traits a second time against a real database rather than against a hash map held in process memory.

We are going to write reversible migrations, create an asynchronous connection pool, and adopt the macros that verify our SQL against a live schema while the project compiles. Our order placement then becomes a genuine transaction, since reserving stock and recording an order must either both succeed or both fail together. Password hashing with Argon2 closes the chapter, along with the reason it must never run directly on our asynchronous runtime.

Preparing PostgreSQL Schema

Writing Reversible Migrations

Our schema evolves throughout the life of an application, and a migration tool records each change as an ordered, repeatable step. The sqlx-cli binary we installed earlier manages that sequence for us, and every migration it generates carries a timestamp prefix so the ordering never depends on filenames chosen by hand. We ask for reversible migrations, which produce a matching pair of files rather than a single one, since the ability to step backwards matters during a failed deployment.

```
sqlx database create
sqlx migrate add -r create_catalogue
```

Our command creates two empty files under a **migrations** directory, one describing the change and one undoing it. We open the upward file first and define the tables that hold our catalogue and our accounts.

```
CREATE TYPE order_status AS ENUM (
    'pending', 'paid', 'packed', 'shipped', 'delivered',
'cancelled'
);


CREATE TABLE books (
    id              UUID PRIMARY KEY DEFAULT gen_random_uuid(),
    isbn            TEXT NOT NULL UNIQUE,
    title           TEXT NOT NULL,
```

```
    author          TEXT NOT NULL,
    price_cents     BIGINT NOT NULL CHECK (price_cents >= 0),
    stock           INTEGER NOT NULL DEFAULT 0 CHECK (stock >= 0),
    published_on    TIMESTAMPTZ NOT NULL
);

CREATE TABLE users (
    id              UUID PRIMARY KEY DEFAULT gen_random_uuid(),
    email           TEXT NOT NULL UNIQUE,
    display_name    TEXT NOT NULL,
    password_hash   TEXT NOT NULL,
    created_at      TIMESTAMPTZ NOT NULL DEFAULT now()
);

CREATE INDEX books_author_idx ON books (author);
```

A pair of constraints in that definition enforces rules our Rust code would otherwise carry entirely alone. The check on **stock** makes a negative quantity impossible at the storage layer, so even a defective query cannot corrupt our inventory, and the uniqueness constraint on **isbn** prevents duplicate catalogue entries regardless of which code path performs the insert. A constraint placed here survives every refactoring above it, which makes it considerably more durable than validation written inside a handler.

The downward file reverses each statement in the opposite order, since dependent objects must disappear before the objects they reference. We keep both halves complete rather than leaving the reversal empty, because an irreversible migration removes our only safe route backwards when a release misbehaves in production. Every migration we write from this point onward carries the same discipline, since a schema change without a reversal quietly removes an option we may one day need badly.

```
DROP INDEX IF EXISTS books_author_idx;
DROP TABLE IF EXISTS users;
DROP TABLE IF EXISTS books;
DROP TYPE IF EXISTS order_status;
```

Mapping Domain Enums onto Postgres Types

Our **OrderStatus** enumeration exists in the domain crate, and PostgreSQL now holds a matching type of its own. The obvious move would attach a **sqlx::Type** derive to the domain enumeration directly, and we deliberately decline that shortcut. We established earlier that our domain crate depends on no database driver, and a concrete reason now becomes visible, since that crate also compiles to WebAssembly for the browser where a Postgres driver has no meaning whatsoever. That constraint now earns its keep.

We therefore introduce a new workspace member that owns every database concern, and both backends depend on it rather than on sqlx directly. Our **persistence** crate holds the pool, the queries, and the small amount of mapping that the boundary requires.

```
cargo new --lib persistence
```

Our new crate declares an enumeration mirroring the domain one, carries the sqlx derive, and converts in both directions.

```
use domain::models::OrderStatus;


#[derive(Debug, Clone, Copy, sqlx::Type)]
#[sqlx(type_name = "order_status", rename_all = "snake_case")]
pub enum DbOrderStatus {
    Pending, Paid, Packed, Shipped, Delivered, Cancelled,
}


impl From<DbOrderStatus> for OrderStatus {
    fn from(value: DbOrderStatus) -> Self {
        match value {
            DbOrderStatus::Pending => OrderStatus::Pending,
            DbOrderStatus::Paid => OrderStatus::Paid,
            DbOrderStatus::Packed => OrderStatus::Packed,
            DbOrderStatus::Shipped => OrderStatus::Shipped,
            DbOrderStatus::Delivered => OrderStatus::Delivered,
            DbOrderStatus::Cancelled => OrderStatus::Cancelled,
        }
    }
}
```

An exhaustive match earns its keep the moment somebody adds a variant to either side. A new status in the domain enumeration breaks this conversion at compile time, which forces a matching migration rather than allowing a silent mismatch between our code and our schema. Any blanket conversion built from string names would compile happily and then fail at runtime against a database that had never heard of the new value.

Running Migrations at Startup

We may run migrations from the command line during development, and our application should also apply them on startup so that a freshly deployed container reaches a usable state without any manual intervention. The **sqlx::migrate!** macro embeds every file into the binary at compile time, which means our deployment artifact carries its own schema history and needs no accompanying files travelling beside it. Our container image therefore stays self-sufficient, which matters considerably for the deployment work ahead.

```
pub async fn run_migrations(pool: &PgPool) -> Result<(),
DomainError> {

    sqlx::migrate!("./migrations")

        .run(pool)

        .await

        .map_err(|e| DomainError::Storage(Box::new(e)))

}
```

We can now apply the schema from the command line before the first build.

```
sqlx migrate run
```

The tool reports each migration as it applies, and a second invocation reports nothing because everything already exists.

```
Applied 20260727094512/migrate create catalogue (18.442ms)
```

The migrator records every applied migration in a tracking table and skips anything already present, so repeated startups stay entirely harmless. A simultaneous startup also stays safe, because the migrator takes an advisory lock before examining that table and releases it afterwards. Several replicas launching together will therefore serialize naturally, with one applying the change while the others wait and then discover nothing left to do. At no point does our own coordination become necessary.

Connecting through Async Pool

Creating and Configuring Pool

A connection pool keeps a set of open connections ready for reuse, since establishing a PostgreSQL connection involves a network round trip and an authentication exchange that we would rather not repeat thousands of times per minute. Our pool reads its address from the DATABASE_URL variable we placed in the environment file earlier, and we set explicit bounds rather than accepting whatever defaults happen to apply on a given machine. Bounds stated outright make our behaviour predictable.

```
use std::time::Duration;

use sqlx::postgres::{PgPool, PgPoolOptions};


pub async fn connect(database_url: &str) -> Result<PgPool,
DomainError> {

    PgPoolOptions::new()

        .max_connections(20)

        .min_connections(2)

        .acquire_timeout(Duration::from_secs(5))

        .idle_timeout(Duration::from_secs(600))

        .test_before_acquire(true)

        .connect(database_url)

        .await

        .map_err(|e| DomainError::Storage(Box::new(e)))

}
```

Here, the **`acquire_timeout`** setting matters considerably more than the maximum size does. Lacking it, a request arriving while every connection is busy waits indefinitely, and the queue grows until the whole application becomes unresponsive to everybody. A five-second bound instead converts that condition into a prompt failure that our error mapping already handles, and the resulting alert points at database saturation rather than at some unrelated symptom noticed much later. That prompt failure beats slow degradation every time.

The pool size deserves a brief warning, because larger is frequently worse rather than better. Every connection consumes a backend process on the PostgreSQL side, and a pool exceeding what the database can comfortably serve merely moves the queue from our application into the server itself. We measure that relationship properly with real figures later, though twenty connections per instance suits our development work and most modest deployments perfectly well. Any increase should follow a measurement rather than precede one.

Replacing In-memory Implementations

Our application state gains a pool and loses two hash maps, and the change touches exactly one line in each backend. We built our state around AppState with an Arc per service, then wrapped the identical structure in **web::Data** for the second backend, so neither arrangement needs revisiting here at all. Here, we simply construct the Postgres implementations instead of the in-memory ones and hand them to the state exactly as before.

```
use persistence::{connect, run_migrations, PgAccounts,
PgInventory, PgOrders};


impl AppState {

    pub async fn new(leptos_options: LeptosOptions) ->
Result<Self, DomainError> {

        let pool =
connect(&std::env::var("DATABASE_URL").expect("DATABASE_URL"))

            .await?;

        run_migrations(&pool).await?;


        Ok(Self {

            leptos_options,

            inventory: Arc::new(PgInventory::new(pool.clone())),

            orders: Arc::new(PgOrders::new(pool.clone())),

            accounts: Arc::new(PgAccounts::new(pool)),

            jwt_secret:
Arc::new(std::env::var("JWT_SECRET").expect("JWT_SECRET")),

        })

    }

}
```

Our three pool clones cost almost nothing, because **PgPool** holds its connections behind a shared handle and every clone points at the identical underlying set. All three implementations therefore draw from one pool rather than opening three separate ones, which keeps total connection usage predictable no matter how many services we eventually add to the state as the application grows. A single shared pool also means our tuning applies uniformly rather than being divided three ways.

Not another line in either backend changes at all. Our handlers, routes, middleware, and error mapping all stay untouched, because every one of them was written against the traits declared earlier rather than against any particular implementation. That outcome is the payment we collect for the architectural discipline of the earlier chapters, and it arrives exactly where the design predicted that it would. Very few architectural promises ever repay themselves quite so visibly as this one.

Writing Compile-time Checked Queries

Verifying Queries against Live Schema

The sqlx macros perform something unusual among database libraries, since they connect to a real database while our project compiles, and verify every query against the actual schema.

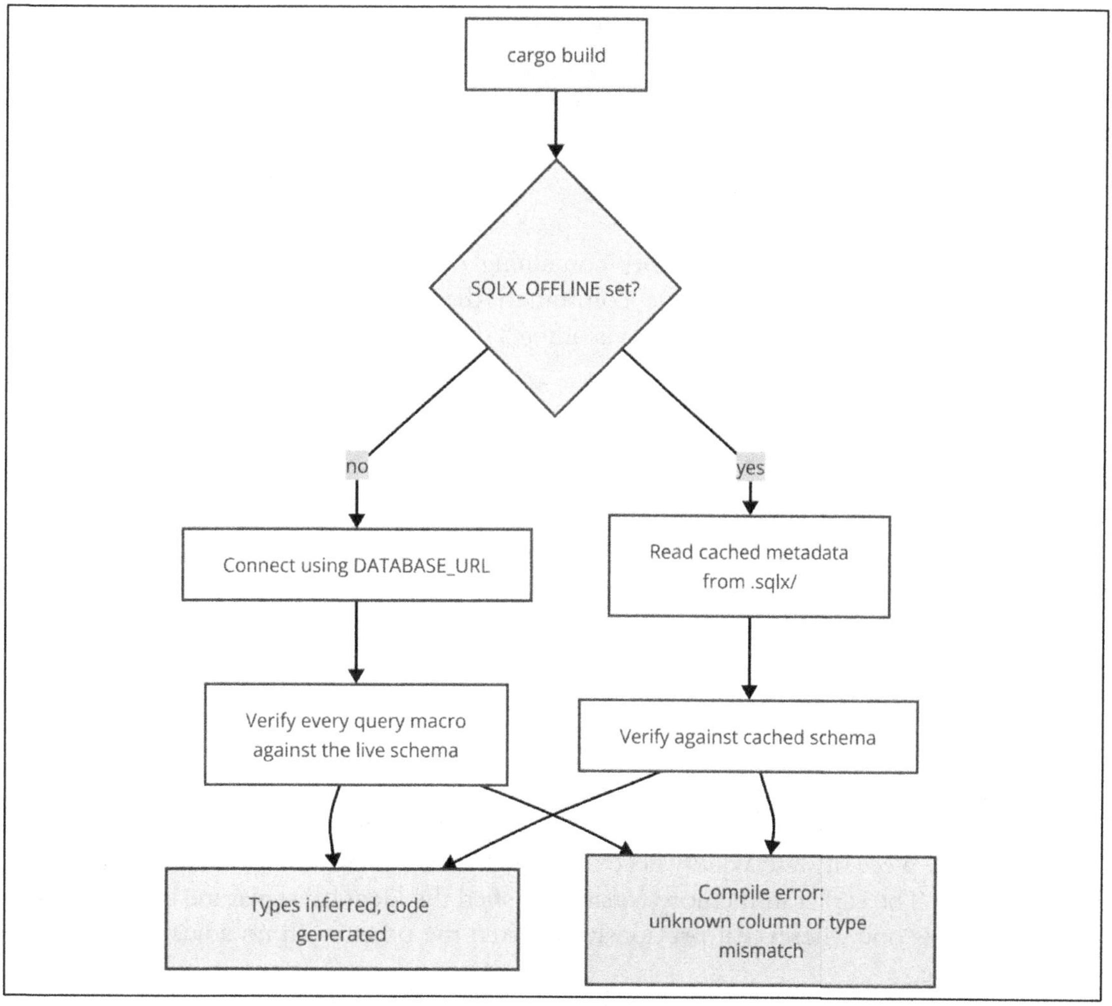

A misspelled column, a type mismatch, or an incorrect parameter quantity becomes a compile error rather than a runtime failure discovered later by a visitor. Our SQL therefore receives the same scrutiny that our Rust receives, which removes an entire category of defect that ordinarily reaches production unnoticed. That verification needs DATABASE_URL at compile time, and the variable already sits in our environment file from the outset.

Our first compilation after a schema change may therefore fail until the migration runs, which sounds inconvenient and is in fact the mechanism working exactly as intended. A build that succeeds against an unmigrated database would simply defer the same failure until a request arrived, and defects always cost less when caught earlier.

Preparing Offline Query Data

A live database requirement at compile time would break our release pipeline and any build running on a machine without PostgreSQL installed. The **cargo sqlx prepare** command solves that by extracting the verification metadata into a directory we commit alongside the code, and builds then verify against that cached description rather than against a running server. Our verification loses nothing in the exchange, since the cached description reflects the very schema our migrations produced.

```
cargo sqlx prepare --workspace
```

Our command writes a **sqlx** directory containing one JSON file per distinct query. We commit that directory, exactly as we committed the lockfile earlier, so anyone cloning LibroCommerce can build it without provisioning a database first.

```
git add .sqlx
git commit -m "Add offline query metadata"
```

A failure to regenerate that data after a query change produces a confusing build error, so the habit matters considerably. Any build with SQLX_OFFLINE set reports that a query is missing from the cache, and the remedy is always the same single command. We add a check to our pipeline later that regenerates the metadata and fails whenever the result differs from what we committed, which catches the omission before a merge rather than afterwards.

Implementing InventoryService over Postgres

We are now ready to satisfy our first trait against real storage, and the signatures come straight from our earlier traits without any alteration. Our implementation holds the pool and nothing else, since every piece of state a query needs arrives through its parameters rather than through the struct itself. The earlier in-memory version satisfied the identical signature, so the compiler now accepts this one wherever it previously accepted the other, with no adjustment required anywhere above.

```
use domain::models::{Book, BookFilter};
```

```
use domain::services::InventoryService;
use domain::DomainError;
use sqlx::postgres::PgPool;
use uuid::Uuid;

pub struct PgInventory {
    pool: PgPool,
}

impl PgInventory {
    pub fn new(pool: PgPool) -> Self {
        Self { pool }
    }
}

impl InventoryService for PgInventory {
    #[tracing::instrument(skip(self), fields(book_count))]
    async fn list_books(&self, filter: BookFilter) ->
Result<Vec<Book>, DomainError> {
        let books = sqlx::query_as!(
            Book,
            r#"
            SELECT id, isbn, title, author, price_cents, stock,
published_on
            FROM books
            WHERE ($1::TEXT IS NULL OR author = $1)
              AND ($2::TEXT IS NULL OR title ILIKE '%' || $2 ||
'%')
              AND (NOT $3::BOOLEAN OR stock > 0)
            ORDER BY title
            LIMIT $4 OFFSET $5
            "#,
```

```
            filter.author,
            filter.search,
            filter.in_stock_only,
            filter.limit.clamp(1, 100),
            filter.offset.max(0),
        )
        .fetch_all(&self.pool)
        .await
        .map_err(storage)?;

        tracing::Span::current().record("book_count",
books.len());
        Ok(books)
    }
}
```

That query handles optional filters through a pattern well worth remembering, where each condition passes automatically whenever its parameter is null. A single prepared statement therefore serves every combination of filters, and PostgreSQL reuses its execution plan rather than parsing a freshly assembled string on each request. Any concatenated string would also invite injection, whereas a bound parameter can never be interpreted as SQL under any circumstances at all. Here, safety and performance align neatly.

Our **`limit`** value passes through **`clamp`** before reaching the query, which prevents a client from requesting the entire catalogue inside one response. We established earlier that extractors validate shapes, and this bound complements that work by restricting magnitude rather than form. A request asking for a thousand rows quietly receives a hundred instead, and our database never faces an unbounded scan produced by a careless or deliberately hostile caller. Every listing endpoint deserves such a ceiling.

Composing Transactions for Orders

Placing Order Atomically

An order placement changes several tables at once, and a partial success would leave our data inconsistent in ways nobody notices immediately. A stock reservation without a recorded order silently loses inventory, while a recorded order without a reservation oversells the book to somebody. One transaction binds both changes into a single unit, so the database either applies everything or applies nothing at all, and no intermediate state ever becomes visible. That all-or-nothing property is precisely what a transaction buys us.

```
impl OrderService for PgOrders {
    #[tracing::instrument(skip(self, lines))]
    async fn place_order(
        &self,
        user_id: Uuid,
        lines: Vec<OrderLine>,
    ) -> Result<Order, DomainError> {
        let mut tx = self.pool.begin().await.map_err(storage)?;

        let order_id: Uuid = sqlx::query_scalar!(
            "INSERT INTO orders (user_id, status) VALUES ($1,
'pending') RETURNING id",
            user_id
        )
        .fetch_one(&mut *tx)
        .await
        .map_err(storage)?;

        for line in &lines {
            let remaining: Option<i32> = sqlx::query_scalar!(
                r#"
                UPDATE books SET stock = stock - $1
                WHERE id = $2 AND stock >= $1
                RETURNING stock
                "#,
                line.quantity,
                line.book_id,
            )
```

```
        .fetch_optional(&mut *tx)
        .await
        .map_err(storage)?;

        if remaining.is_none() {
            tx.rollback().await.map_err(storage)?;
            return Err(DomainError::InsufficientStock {
                id: line.book_id,
                available:
self.current_stock(line.book_id).await?,
            });
        }

        sqlx::query!(
            r#"
            INSERT INTO order_lines (order_id, book_id,
quantity, unit_price_cents)
            VALUES ($1, $2, $3, $4)
            "#,
            order_id, line.book_id, line.quantity,
line.unit_price_cents,
        )
        .execute(&mut *tx)
        .await
        .map_err(storage)?;
    }

    tx.commit().await.map_err(storage)?;
    self.find_order(order_id).await
  }
}
```

The stock update carries the most important idea in this entire chapter. Our statement decrements the quantity and checks availability within one single operation, because **`stock >= $1`** sits inside the same **`UPDATE`** that performs the subtraction. A read of the stock followed by a separate decision would open a window where two concurrent orders both observe sufficient inventory and both proceed, which oversells the book. The row stays locked for the duration of that update, so the second order finds a reduced figure and matches no rows.

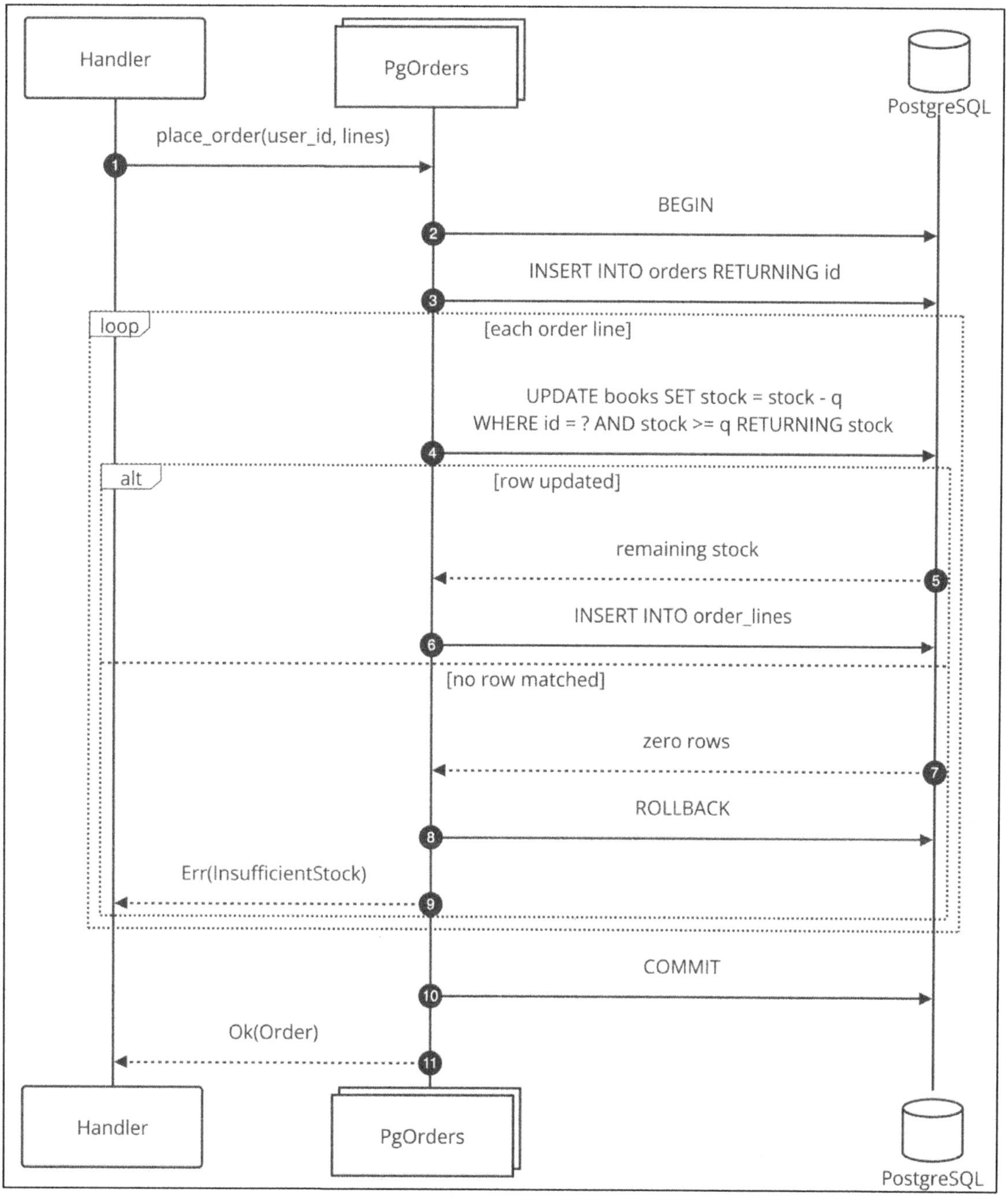

Our transaction also guards against failures we never anticipated at all. An error returned by the **?** operator drops the transaction handle without committing it, and sqlx issues a rollback automatically during that drop. A panic produces the same outcome, so no code path whatsoever can leave a transaction hanging open, and our inventory stays consistent even when something unexpected interrupts the sequence partway through.

Enforcing Status Lifecycle

We declared earlier that advance_status rejects transitions the lifecycle forbids, and the diagram there recorded precisely which moves we permit. Our implementation reads the current value, consults that rule, and updates only when the requested move is legal. Both steps live inside one transaction so that two concurrent updates cannot each observe the original status and then both proceed to change it.

```
fn allows(from: OrderStatus, to: OrderStatus) -> bool {
    use OrderStatus::*;
    matches!(
        (from, to),
        (Pending, Paid) | (Pending, Cancelled)
            | (Paid, Packed) | (Paid, Cancelled)
            | (Packed, Shipped)
            | (Shipped, Delivered)
    )
}


async fn advance_status(&self, id: Uuid, next: OrderStatus) ->
Result<Order, DomainError> {
    let mut tx = self.pool.begin().await.map_err(storage)?;

    let current: DbOrderStatus = sqlx::query_scalar!(
        r#"SELECT status AS "status: DbOrderStatus" FROM orders
WHERE id = $1 FOR UPDATE"#,
        id
    )
    .fetch_optional(&mut *tx)
    .await
```

```
    .map_err(storage)?
    .ok_or(DomainError::OrderNotFound(id))?;

    let from: OrderStatus = current.into();
    if !allows(from, next) {
        return Err(DomainError::InvalidTransition { order: id,
from, to: next });
    }

    sqlx::query!(
        r#"UPDATE orders SET status = $1 WHERE id = $2"#,
        DbOrderStatus::from(next) as DbOrderStatus,
        id
    )
    .execute(&mut *tx)
    .await
    .map_err(storage)?;

    tx.commit().await.map_err(storage)?;
    self.find_order(id).await
}
```

A pair of syntactic details there belongs to the macros rather than to SQL itself. The **AS "status: DbOrderStatus"** annotation tells sqlx which Rust type a column maps onto, since a custom Postgres type gives the macro no way to infer that on its own. Its trailing as DbOrderStatus on the bind parameter performs the identical service in the opposite direction, and omitting either one produces a type error naming the column involved. Both annotations repay a moment's attention.

The **FOR UPDATE** clause completes our protection by locking the selected row until the transaction ends. A second request attempting the same transition waits at that lock rather than reading a stale status, and it then observes the updated value and fails the rule check exactly as it should. The lock and the rule must work together here, since neither one alone prevents a concurrent double transition. Very rarely does a single mechanism make concurrent behaviour correct.

Translating SQL Failures into Domain Errors

Our conversions run through a small helper rather than through a trait implementation, and the reason returns to the boundary we drew earlier. An **`impl From<sqlx::Error> for DomainError`** requires one of the two types to belong to the crate declaring it, which would force sqlx into the domain crate and undo the portability established a moment ago. A plain function inside the persistence crate achieves the same convenience without any of that cost.

```
pub(crate) fn storage(err: sqlx::Error) -> DomainError {
    DomainError::Storage(Box::new(err))
}

pub(crate) fn account_error(err: sqlx::Error) -> DomainError {
    if let sqlx::Error::Database(db) = &err {
        if db.code().as_deref() == Some("23505") {
            return DomainError::DuplicateEmail;
        }
    }
    storage(err)
}
```

The distinction between a duplicate email and a general failure change what a visitor experiences quite considerably. Error code 23505 identifies a unique constraint violation, and recognizing it lets our registration endpoint report that the address is already registered rather than returning an opaque internal failure. Our domain enumeration gains one variant to carry that meaning, and Chapter 3 and 4 both map it onto a conflict response without any further work from us. A single variant therefore carries real value.

Every other database failure stays anonymous quite deliberately, and we explained earlier why a storage message never reaches a client directly. What matters here is that the decision about which failures deserve individual treatment belongs to the persistence layer, since only that layer can interpret a driver code at all. Our web layers receive a domain error they already understand and need no knowledge of PostgreSQL whatsoever. The reading of a failure belongs wherever the knowledge to read it already lives.

Hashing Passwords with Argon2

Registering and Storing Credentials

Our accounts table holds a **password_hash** column and never a password, since credentials kept in recoverable form turn any database disclosure into an immediate compromise of every account we hold. The Argon2 algorithm derives a hash that resists both brute force and purpose-built hardware, because it deliberately consumes memory as well as processor time. That crate, pinned at the outset, implements the variant currently recommended for password storage. Storage that can be reversed is simply never acceptable for a credential.

```
use argon2::password_hash::{rand_core::OsRng, PasswordHasher,
SaltString};

use argon2::{Argon2, PasswordHash, PasswordVerifier};


pub fn hash_password(password: &str) -> Result<String,
DomainError> {

    let salt = SaltString::generate(&mut OsRng);

    Argon2::default()

        .hash_password(password.as_bytes(), &salt)

        .map(|hash| hash.to_string())

        .map_err(|e| DomainError::Storage(Box::new(e)))

}
```

A fresh salt accompanies every password, and the resulting string carries that salt alongside the algorithm parameters and the digest itself. Two accounts sharing an identical password therefore produce entirely different stored values, which defeats any precomputed lookup and forces an attacker to attack each account separately. The parameters stored inside that string also let us strengthen them later without invalidating existing hashes, since verification reads whatever settings each record actually used.

Verifying Passwords without Blocking Runtime

The algorithm is designed to be slow, and that deliberate property creates a hazard on an asynchronous runtime. Our hashing call occupies its thread for tens of milliseconds without ever yielding, while an asynchronous executor assumes that every task yields promptly. A handful of simultaneous logins would therefore stall unrelated requests sharing the same worker thread, which turns a security feature into an availability problem precisely when traffic is heaviest. Our remedy below moves that work elsewhere entirely.

```
impl AccountService for PgAccounts {

    #[tracing::instrument(skip(self, password))]

    async fn authenticate(&self, email: String, password: String)
```

```
    -> Result<User, DomainError>
    {
        let record = sqlx::query!(
            r#"SELECT id, email, display_name, created_at,
password_hash
               FROM users WHERE email = $1"#,
            email
        )
        .fetch_optional(&self.pool)
        .await
        .map_err(storage)?
        .ok_or(DomainError::InvalidCredentials)?;

        let stored = record.password_hash.clone();
        let valid = tokio::task::spawn_blocking(move || {
            let parsed = PasswordHash::new(&stored).ok()?;
            Some(Argon2::default()
                .verify_password(password.as_bytes(), &parsed)
                .is_ok())
        })
        .await
        .map_err(|e| DomainError::Storage(Box::new(e)))?
        .unwrap_or(false);

        if !valid {
            return Err(DomainError::InvalidCredentials);
        }

        Ok(User {
            id: record.id,
            email: record.email,
```

```
            display_name: record.display_name,
            created_at: record.created_at,
        })
    }
}
```

Our **spawn_blocking** call moves the expensive work onto a separate thread pool reserved for exactly this purpose, and the asynchronous worker stays free to serve other requests while it runs. An operation consuming more than roughly a hundred microseconds of uninterrupted processor time belongs on that pool, which includes image processing, compression, and certain parsing work alongside our password hashing here. Work shorter than that rough threshold runs perfectly well on the asynchronous worker itself without any special handling.

Our decision to return **InvalidCredentials** for both a missing account and a wrong password is equally deliberate. Separate messages would let anybody probe which addresses hold accounts, turning our login endpoint into a directory of our entire user base. An identical response for both conditions closes that avenue completely, and we add rate limiting later so that repeated attempts become expensive as well as uninformative. We give up nothing at all by staying silent about which accounts exist.

Summary

We replaced our in-memory storage with PostgreSQL and neither backend required a single change, which settles the promise that both Chapter 3 and Chapter 4 ended upon. Our reversible migrations now define the schema, our constraints enforce rules at the storage layer, and a new **persistence** crate holds every database concern so the domain crate stays portable enough to compile for the browser. The mapping of enumerations across that boundary costs a few lines and preserves the separation entirely.

We then adopted the sqlx macros that verify SQL against a live schema during compilation, committed the offline metadata so builds need no database, and wrote transactional order placement where one conditional update prevents overselling under concurrency. Our status transitions hold a row lock while consulting the lifecycle rule, and our password hashing runs on a blocking pool rather than stalling the runtime. In Chapter 6, we expose this storage through REST, GraphQL, and OAuth, and every one of those interfaces draws on the layer we just built.

Chapter 6
Modern Interactions with REST, GraphQL and OAuth

We will now turn the endpoints built across Chapter 3 and 4 into interfaces that outside clients can rely upon, which is a considerably different undertaking from merely making them work. Our own frontend tolerates a breaking change because we deploy both halves together, whereas a mobile application or a partner integration simply cannot. Every decision in this chapter therefore concerns contracts, stability, and the cost of changing our mind later. A contract outlives the code that produces it.

We are going to add versioning, pagination, and conditional requests to our REST surface, then publish a GraphQL schema that lets clients request precisely the fields they need and nothing else. Our final section replaces the password login with delegated authentication through GitHub, using the authorization code flow with proof key protection. Both backends receive each addition, though the second one costs us very little once the first already exists.

Designing Public REST Surface

Versioning and Stable Contracts

Our published interface acquires clients we cannot contact, and those clients break whenever a field disappears or quietly changes meaning. A versioning scheme buys us the freedom to evolve without stranding anybody, and a path prefix remains the plainest approach available to us. Our existing routes move beneath **/api/v1**, which costs one line in each backend and immediately reserves room for whatever eventually follows it. Not one of our existing clients notices anything on the day we add it.

```
Router::new()
    .nest("/api/v1", v1_routes())
    .nest("/api/v2", v2_routes())
```

A purely additive change needs no new version at all, and the ability to recognize such a change saves considerable effort over time. New optional fields, new endpoints, and new enumeration variants that older clients may safely ignore all stay compatible. Any removal, rename, type change, or newly required parameter breaks somebody, and each of those belongs in a fresh version. Our serde attributes make the safe direction explicit, so a client parsing our responses tolerates fields it has never encountered before.

```
#[derive(Debug, Serialize)]
pub struct BookResponse {
    pub id: Uuid,
    pub title: String,
    pub author: String,
```

```
    pub price_cents: i64,
    #[serde(skip_serializing_if = "Option::is_none")]
    pub cover_url: Option<String>,
}
```

Our response type sits in the web layer rather than in the domain crate, and that separation earns its keep here for a second reason beyond portability. A domain model serialized directly becomes a published contract by accident, so every internal refactoring then risks breaking a client we cannot reach. An explicit response type instead lets our internal structures change freely while the transmitted shape stays exactly where we put it, and the conversion between them stops compiling whenever the two drift apart.

Paginating Large Collections

We clamped our query limit to a hundred rows earlier, and that ceiling now needs a companion so clients can retrieve everything through successive requests. Our envelope carries the items alongside enough metadata for a caller to know whether more remain unfetched. A total tally would settle that question directly, though it costs a second query against the same table, so we return a cursor and a simple flag instead.

```
#[derive(Debug, Serialize)]
pub struct Page<T> {
    pub items: Vec<T>,
    pub next_cursor: Option<String>,
    pub has_more: bool,
}

pub async fn list_books(
    State(state): State<AppState>,
    Query(params): Query<PageParams>,
) -> Result<Json<Page<BookResponse>>, ApiError> {
    let mut filter = params.into_filter();
    filter.limit += 1;

    let mut books = state.inventory.list_books(filter).await?;
    let has_more = books.len() as i64 > params.limit;
```

```
    books.truncate(params.limit as usize);

    Ok(Json(Page {
        next_cursor: has_more.then(||
encode_cursor(books.last())),
        has_more,
        items:
books.into_iter().map(BookResponse::from).collect(),
    }))
}
```

A request for one row beyond the limit is a small trick well worth keeping. Our query returns either the requested quantity or one extra row, and the presence of that extra row tells us more results exist without any separate counting query running against the database. We then discard it before responding, so the client receives exactly what it asked for while we learn something the client genuinely needs to know. A single extra row settles the question.

A cursor also behaves correctly under concurrent writes, which an offset does not. Any book inserted while a client walks the catalogue shifts every subsequent offset by one position, so that client either sees a duplicate entry or misses one entirely. One anchored to the last item returned stays stable regardless of insertions elsewhere in the table, and our query already sorts by title, which gives us a natural anchor for exactly that cursor.

Conditional Requests with ETags

Our catalogue changes infrequently while clients poll it regularly, and conditional requests let both sides avoid transferring data that has not actually changed. The response carries a validator, the client returns that validator on its next request, and we reply with an empty body whenever nothing has moved since. Both the bandwidth and the parsing time disappear entirely for the common case, which is by far the most frequent one. Our catalogue endpoints benefit most from this.

```
use axum::http::{header, HeaderMap, StatusCode};

pub async fn find_book(
    State(state): State<AppState>,
    Path(id): Path<Uuid>,
    headers: HeaderMap,
) -> Result<Response, ApiError> {
```

```
    let book = state.inventory.find_book(id).await?;
    let etag = format!("\"{:x}\"",
Sha256::digest(book.updated_at.to_rfc3339()));

    if headers
        .get(header::IF_NONE_MATCH)
        .and_then(|v| v.to_str().ok())
        .is_some_and(|v| v == etag)
    {
        return Ok(StatusCode::NOT_MODIFIED.into_response());
    }

    Ok(([(header::ETAG, etag)],
Json(BookResponse::from(book))).into_response())
}
```

Our validator derives from a timestamp rather than from the serialized body, and that choice matters for consistency across deployments. A hash of the response would change whenever we altered the response type, invalidating every cached copy during an otherwise unrelated release. One drawn from the record instead changes only when the record itself changes, which is precisely the semantics any client expects from a validator it has stored.

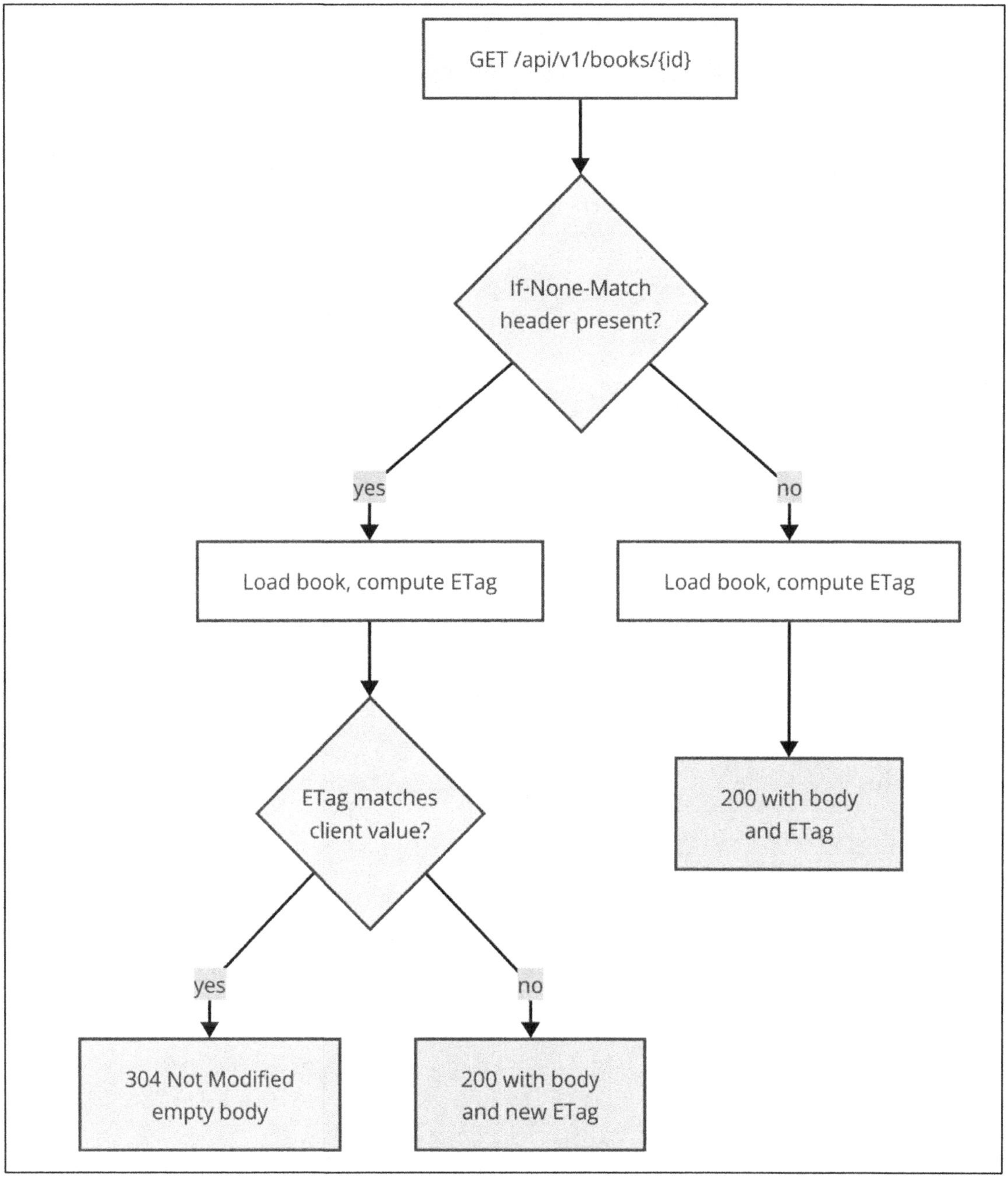

Worth noticing is that we still load the book before deciding, so the database work happens regardless of the outcome. A conditional request saves transfer and parsing rather than query time, and an application needing to save the query as well stores the validator separately inside a cache. We introduce Redis for exactly that kind of work later, where a validator lookup settles the conditional request without ever touching PostgreSQL at all. Our present arrangement saves the smaller cost.

Reporting Problems with RFC 9457

Our error responses currently carry a single message field, which serves our own frontend adequately and serves an outside client rather poorly. A published interface benefits enormously from a documented error format, and RFC 9457 defines one that many clients already understand without any prompting from us. Our bodies gain a type identifier, a title, a status, and whatever extension members a particular failure needs to carry. Those extensions turn a message into usable data.

```
#[derive(Debug, Serialize)]
pub struct ProblemDetails {
    #[serde(rename = "type")]
    pub kind: String,
    pub title: String,
    pub status: u16,
    #[serde(skip_serializing_if = "Option::is_none")]
    pub detail: Option<String>,
    #[serde(flatten)]
    pub extensions: serde_json::Map<String, serde_json::Value>,
}

impl From<&DomainError> for ProblemDetails {
    fn from(err: &DomainError) -> Self {
        match err {
            DomainError::InsufficientStock { id, available } =>
ProblemDetails {
                kind:
"https://librocommerce.example/problems/insufficient-
stock".into(),
                title: "Insufficient stock".into(),
                status: 409,
                detail: Some(err.to_string()),
                extensions: json_map([("book_id", json!(id)),
("available", json!(available))]),
            },
```

```
            other => ProblemDetails::generic(other),
        }
    }
}
```

The extension members carry the real value here rather than the standard fields. Our stock failure reports the remaining quantity as a machine-readable number instead of embedding it inside a sentence, so a client adjusts its request programmatically rather than parsing English. The type field also gives us a stable identifier that survives any rewording of the title, which means client logic keyed on that identifier never breaks when we later improve our messages.

Our responses set a content type of **`application/problem+json`** so clients distinguish an error body from a successful one without inspecting the status code a second time. That change touches only the response construction in each backend, since Chapter 3 and 4 both funnel every failure through a single conversion point. A single edit per backend therefore upgrades every endpoint at once, which is the dividend of having centralized that mapping much earlier. Earlier discipline keeps paying here.

Exposing GraphQL Schema

Defining Object Types with 'async-graphql'

Our REST surface returns fixed shapes, and a client needing three fields from a book still receives all seven of them. That arrangement inverts under GraphQL, where the client specifies exactly which fields it wants, which suits mobile applications on constrained connections particularly well. The **`async-graphql`** crate builds a schema from ordinary Rust types, and our pinned version differs substantially from the release the first edition used. Nearly every schema definition from that release needed rewriting.

Our GraphQL types wrap the domain models rather than deriving directly upon them, for the reason we set out when introducing the persistence crate. A wrapper also lets us expose computed fields that have no storage behind them at all, which turns a constraint into a genuine advantage. Our schema therefore describes what clients should see rather than what our database happens to store, and those two shapes diverge more often than they coincide.

```
use async_graphql::{Context, Object, Result as GqlResult, ID};
use domain::models::Book;

pub struct BookNode(pub Book);
```

```
#[Object]
impl BookNode {
    async fn id(&self) -> ID {
        ID(self.0.id.to_string())
    }

    async fn title(&self) -> &str {
        &self.0.title
    }

    async fn author(&self) -> &str {
        &self.0.author
    }

    async fn price(&self) -> String {
        format!("{}.{:02}", self.0.price_cents / 100,
self.0.price_cents % 100)
    }

    async fn in_stock(&self) -> bool {
        self.0.stock > 0
    }
}
```

A pair of fields there exists only within the schema and nowhere else. Our **price** field formats an integer into a decimal string for display, and our **in_stock** field derives a boolean from a quantity we deliberately choose not to publish. A stock level made public would tell a competitor exactly how our inventory moves, so the schema answers the question a shopper genuinely asks while withholding the figure a rival would want. The design of a schema is therefore a security decision.

Composing Queries and Mutations with MergedObject

A schema grows unwieldy when every query lives inside one enormous type, so we split ours by service area and merge the pieces afterwards. Our derive collects several independent types into a single root, and each area keeps its own file exactly as our domain modules do. A growing schema then costs us a new file rather than an edit to a shared one, which keeps conflicts rare on a team.

```
use async_graphql::{EmptySubscription, MergedObject, Schema};


#[derive(Default)]

pub struct BookQuery;


#[Object]

impl BookQuery {

    async fn book(&self, ctx: &Context<'_>, id: ID) ->
GqlResult<Option<BookNode>> {

        let inventory = ctx.data::<Arc<PgInventory>>()?;

        let uuid = Uuid::parse_str(&id)?;

        Ok(inventory.find_book(uuid).await.ok().map(BookNode))

    }

}


#[derive(MergedObject, Default)]

pub struct Query(BookQuery, OrderQuery);


#[derive(MergedObject, Default)]

pub struct Mutation(OrderMutation);


pub type LibroSchema = Schema<Query, Mutation,
EmptySubscription>;
```

Our schema builder attaches shared values and applies two limits that matter enormously for any public endpoint. A depth limit rejects deeply nested queries, while a complexity limit rejects excessively broad ones, because GraphQL lets a single request demand an enormous amount of work through nesting that looks entirely innocuous on the page. Both limits belong on every public schema, since neither costs anything measurable during normal operation and both prevent a trivially cheap denial of service.

```
pub fn build_schema(state: &AppState) -> LibroSchema {
    Schema::build(Query::default(), Mutation::default(),
EmptySubscription)
        .data(state.inventory.clone())

.data(DataLoader::new(BookLoader::new(state.inventory.clone()),
tokio::spawn))
        .limit_depth(10)
        .limit_complexity(200)
        .finish()
}
```

Lacking those two limits, a caller nests a relationship back upon itself a dozen times and our server performs exponential work for one very small request. A query of that shape needs no malice whatsoever to appear, since a generated client or an experimenting developer produces one entirely by accident. Both limits reject the request before execution even begins, which costs the caller a clear error message and costs us almost nothing at all. We reject far more cheaply than we execute.

Solving N+1 Problem with DataLoader

An order exposes its lines, and each line references a book, so a query fetching ten orders with three lines apiece triggers thirty separate book lookups. That pattern carries the name N+1, and it quietly turns a fast query into a slow one as results grow larger. The **DataLoader** type collects every identifier requested during one execution pass and resolves them together in a single batched query. A single round trip therefore replaces thirty of them.

```
use async_graphql::dataloader::Loader;
use std::collections::HashMap;

pub struct BookLoader {
    inventory: Arc<PgInventory>,
}

impl Loader<Uuid> for BookLoader {
    type Value = Book;
    type Error = Arc<DomainError>;
```

```
    async fn load(&self, keys: &[Uuid]) -> Result<HashMap<Uuid,
Book>, Self::Error> {
        self.inventory
            .find_books_by_ids(keys)
            .await
            .map(|books| books.into_iter().map(|b| (b.id,
b)).collect())
            .map_err(Arc::new)
    }
}
```

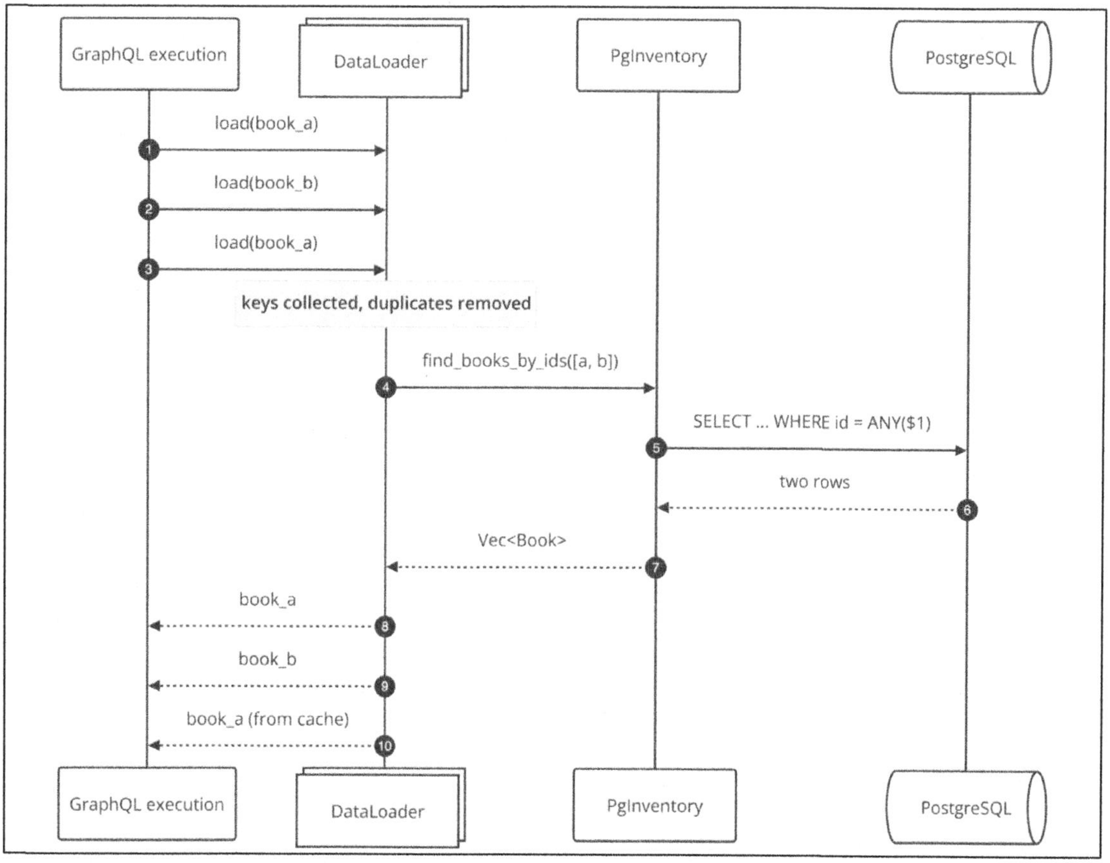

Our loader also removes duplicates before querying, so a book appearing across several orders gets fetched exactly once per request. The underlying query uses **ANY** with an array parameter rather than a generated list of placeholders, which keeps one prepared statement serving any batch size at all. We established earlier that a single prepared statement lets PostgreSQL reuse its execution plan, and that same benefit applies here at a considerably larger scale. The size of a batch stops mattering entirely.

Our resolvers reach the loader through the very same context that carries our services. A resolver needing a book requests it from the loader instead of from the inventory directly, and the batching then happens without that resolver knowing anything whatsoever about it. Our field code therefore stays as simple as a direct lookup would be while performing dramatically better whenever the surrounding query happens to return many rows. We gain performance without any loss of clarity.

Mounting Schema on Both Backends

Both integration crates expose nearly identical request and response types, so mounting the schema costs a handful of lines on either backend. Our Axum route accepts the request, executes it against the schema held in state, and converts the outcome back into a response. Not a line in that handler knows which framework surrounds it, which is why the Actix version below reads identically.

```
use async_graphql_axum::{GraphQLRequest, GraphQLResponse};

pub async fn graphql_handler(
    State(schema): State<LibroSchema>,
    req: GraphQLRequest,
) -> GraphQLResponse {
    schema.execute(req.into_inner()).await.into()
}
```

The Actix equivalent differs only in how the schema arrives, since web::Data replaces the state extractor described earlier. Our handler body stays character for character identical, which is the clearest demonstration yet that the framework boundary sits exactly where we placed it at the start. A single schema drawn from one set of resolvers now serves both frameworks, so any change to that schema reaches both endpoints at the moment we next recompile the workspace.

```
pub async fn graphql_handler(
    schema: web::Data<LibroSchema>,
    req: GraphQLRequest,
) -> GraphQLResponse {
```

```
    schema.execute(req.into_inner()).await.into()
}
```

Our development environment also benefits from an interactive explorer, and the crate ships one needing no build step whatsoever. We serve it at a separate path and disable it outside development, because an exposed explorer advertises our entire schema to anybody who happens to find the endpoint. There is also the option of disabling introspection on the schema builder, which many teams do for production deployments as a matter of routine.

```
use async_graphql::http::GraphiQLSource;


pub async fn graphiql() -> impl IntoResponse {
    Html(GraphiQLSource::build().endpoint("/graphql").finish())
}
```

Authenticating with OAuth2 and GitHub

Configuring oauth2 Client

With delegated authentication, we no longer need to store passwords for visitors who would rather use an account they already hold. Our application never sees the credential at any point, since GitHub authenticates the person and returns a code that we then exchange for a token. The **oauth2** crate reached version 5 with a redesigned builder, and the constructor written for the first edition no longer compiles at all. Our upgrade therefore begins with the client itself.

```
use oauth2::basic::BasicClient;
use oauth2::{AuthUrl, ClientId, ClientSecret, RedirectUrl,
TokenUrl};


pub fn github_client() -> Result<GitHubClient, DomainError> {
    let client =
BasicClient::new(ClientId::new(env_var("GITHUB_CLIENT_ID")?))

.set_client_secret(ClientSecret::new(env_var("GITHUB_CLIENT_SECRE
T")?))
        .set_auth_uri(AuthUrl::new(
```

```
"https://github.com/login/oauth/authorize".to_owned(),
        )?)
        .set_token_uri(TokenUrl::new(
"https://github.com/login/oauth/access_token".to_owned(),
        )?)

.set_redirect_uri(RedirectUrl::new(env_var("OAUTH_REDIRECT_URL")?
)?);

    Ok(client)
}
```

Each endpoint arrives through its own method rather than through positional arguments, and the type system now tracks which endpoints have already been supplied. An attempt to exchange a code before setting the token endpoint fails to compile rather than failing at runtime, because the builder returns a different type at every stage. The fourth version accepted that same mistake happily and reported it only when a visitor first tried to sign in. Detection at compile time is plainly better.

Our HTTP client for the exchange needs one unusual setting worth understanding properly. We must keep redirects disabled throughout, because the token endpoint returns credentials and a redirect could forward those credentials to a location an attacker controls. The timeout below serves the purpose described earlier for outbound calls, and both settings belong on any client that carries secrets. By default, we get neither, so both must be applied deliberately whenever we build such a client.

```
let http_client = reqwest::ClientBuilder::new()
    .redirect(reqwest::redirect::Policy::none())
    .timeout(Duration::from_secs(10))
    .build()?;
```

Redirecting with PKCE and CSRF State

Our sign-in route generates two secrets before sending the visitor away to GitHub. A proof key protects the exchange itself, since an attacker intercepting the returned code cannot use it without holding the matching verifier. The state value protects against cross-site request forgery, because we reject any callback carrying a state value that we never issued ourselves.

Both secrets are generated fresh for every single sign-in attempt, and neither one of them is ever reused afterwards.

```
use oauth2::{CsrfToken, PkceCodeChallenge, Scope};


pub async fn begin_login(State(state): State<AppState>) ->
Result<Redirect, ApiError> {
    let (challenge, verifier) =
PkceCodeChallenge::new_random_sha256();

    let (auth_url, csrf) = state
        .oauth
        .authorize_url(CsrfToken::new_random)
        .add_scope(Scope::new("read:user".to_owned()))
        .add_scope(Scope::new("user:email".to_owned()))
        .set_pkce_challenge(challenge)
        .url();

    state
        .redis
        .set_ex(format!("oauth:{}", csrf.secret()),
verifier.secret(), 600)
        .await?;

    Ok(Redirect::to(auth_url.as_str()))
}
```

Our verifier travels to Redis rather than to the visitor, keyed by the state value and expiring after ten minutes. A cookie would work equally well for this purpose, though the server-side arrangement lets us expire the entry precisely and revoke it whenever needed. We formalize session storage on this same Redis instance later, so our entry becomes an early tenant of infrastructure we provisioned at the outset. No new infrastructure is required at all.

The two scopes we request follow a principle well worth applying everywhere. Our application needs an identity and an email address, so we ask for exactly those two things and nothing whatsoever beyond them. A broader request would present the visitor with an alarming consent screen and would expand our liability considerably if our own token store were ever compromised by somebody. That narrow scope therefore protects the visitor and reduces our own exposure at the very same time.

Exchanging Code for Profile

Our callback receives the code alongside the state, and the first action verifies that state before anything else happens at all. A callback whose state is absent from Redis gets rejected immediately, since either the request is forged or the attempt has already expired. The diagram below traces the complete exchange from the first redirect through to the token we finally issue. Every arrow in it corresponds to code we have either written already or are about to write.

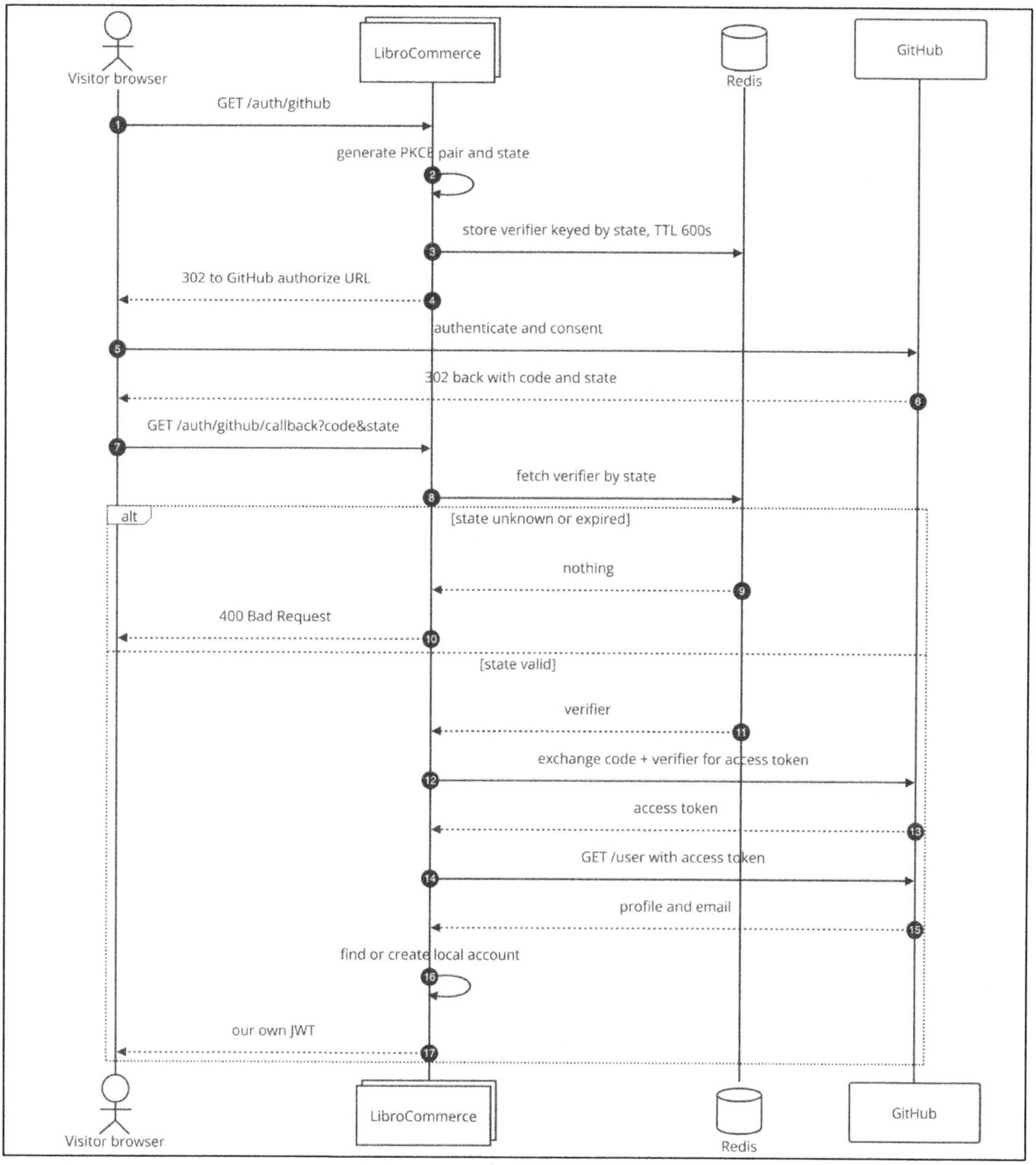


```
pub async fn oauth_callback(
    State(state): State<AppState>,
    Query(params): Query<CallbackParams>,
) -> Result<Json<TokenResponse>, ApiError> {
    let verifier: String = state
```

```
        .redis
        .get_del(format!("oauth:{}", params.state))
        .await?
        .ok_or(DomainError::InvalidCredentials)?;

    let token = state
        .oauth
        .exchange_code(AuthorizationCode::new(params.code))
        .set_pkce_verifier(PkceCodeVerifier::new(verifier))
        .request_async(&state.http)
        .await
        .map_err(|_| DomainError::InvalidCredentials)?;

    let profile = fetch_github_profile(&state.http,
token.access_token()).await?;
    let user = state.accounts.upsert_from_oauth(profile).await?;

    Ok(Json(TokenResponse {
        token: issue_token(&user, &state.jwt_secret)?,
    }))
}
```

Our retrieval uses **get_del** rather than a plain read, which removes the entry at the very moment it returns the value. A replayed callback therefore finds nothing and fails, so a code intercepted from browser history or from a proxy log cannot be exchanged a second time by anybody. One atomic operation buys that protection, whereas a separate read followed by a delete would leave a usable window open between them. The all-or-nothing property matters even here.

Issuing Own Token

The final step converts a GitHub identity into a LibroCommerce account, and our application issues its own token rather than storing the one GitHub returned. We established the claim structure and the signing procedure earlier, and nothing whatsoever about either changes here. What matters is that the GitHub token now stops travelling any further, since it grants access to resources reaching well beyond our own application.

```
impl PgAccounts {
    pub async fn upsert_from_oauth(&self, profile: GitHubProfile)
        -> Result<User, DomainError>
    {
        sqlx::query_as!(
            User,
            r#"
            INSERT INTO users (email, display_name,
password_hash, oauth_provider)
            VALUES ($1, $2, '', 'github')
            ON CONFLICT (email) DO UPDATE SET display_name =
EXCLUDED.display_name
            RETURNING id, email, display_name, created_at
            "#,
            profile.email,
            profile.name.unwrap_or(profile.login),
        )
        .fetch_one(&self.pool)
        .await
        .map_err(storage)
    }
}
```

An upsert handles both new and returning visitors within one statement, which avoids the race that a separate check would otherwise introduce. A pair of simultaneous sign-ins from the same account would find no existing row and both attempt an insert, and the second would then violate our uniqueness constraint. The conflict clause instead updates the display name and returns the existing record, so either path yields a usable account without any special handling. That concurrent case stops being a concern entirely.

Our empty **password_hash** deserves a brief remark, since a blank column looks careless at first sight. The Argon2 algorithm never produces an empty string, so no password can ever verify against that stored value, and an account created through GitHub therefore cannot be reached through the password route. A nullable column would express the same intent more clearly, and either arrangement works provided our verification path treats the absence as a failure.

Summary

We turned working endpoints into published interfaces, which required attention to contracts rather than to mechanics. Our REST surface now carries a version prefix, returns cursor-based collections that stay correct under concurrent writes, honours conditional requests through validators drawn from record timestamps, and reports failures in the format RFC 9457 defines. By keeping response types separate from domain models, we leave our internal structures free to change without ever breaking anyone downstream from us. A contract and an internal structure therefore stay apart.

We then published a GraphQL schema built from wrapper types that expose computed fields and withhold sensitive figures, merged several query roots into one, and guarded the endpoint with depth and complexity limits. A DataLoader collapses the repeated lookups that GraphQL invites, and both backends mount the schema with identical handler bodies. Our OAuth flow now delegates authentication to GitHub with proof key protection and single-use state, issuing our own token at the end. In Chapter 7, we rebuild the frontend against these interfaces.

CHAPTER 7
FRONT-END DEVELOPMENT WITH LEPTOS AND WEBASSEMBLY

We will now build the storefront that visitors actually see, working against the interfaces we published earlier. The first component we wrote proved the toolchain functioned, and the material ahead goes considerably deeper, since a catalogue needs asynchronous loading, client-side routing, reusable components, and forms that survive a failed connection. Every piece compiles to WebAssembly and to native code alike.

We are going to work through the reactive system that makes Leptos updates precise, load remote data through resources guarded by suspense boundaries, declare nested routes for our catalogue, and submit orders through actions that function even without JavaScript. Our closing section measures the bundle we ship and then addresses the maintenance question honestly, because anybody choosing this stack in 2026 deserves an accurate picture rather than an enthusiastic one. An accurate picture serves a decision better than an optimistic one does.

Reactivity in Leptos 0.8

Signals, Memos and Derived Values

Our storefront holds state that changes as visitors interact with it, and Leptos tracks every dependency between that state and the view automatically. A signal holds a value and records which parts of our interface read it, so an update touches only the specific nodes concerned. We introduced the basic pair at the very start, and three further primitives now become useful as our interface grows beyond a single control. Each one addresses a distinct kind of change.

```
use leptos::prelude::*;


let (query, set_query) = signal(String::new());

let filters = RwSignal::new(BookFilter::default());


let trimmed = Memo::new(move |_|
query.get().trim().to_lowercase());

let is_searching = move || !trimmed.get().is_empty();
```

The snippet holds four different constructs, and each serves a distinct purpose. A **`signal`** returns a separate getter and setter, which lets us hand the getter to a child component without granting it permission to modify anything. An **`RwSignal`** combines both halves into one value, which suits state we pass around freely inside a single component. A **`Memo`** caches a computed result and only notifies its dependents when that result actually changes. The choice between them matters for performance.

The final line holds no special type at all, since a plain closure reading a signal already behaves reactively. A closure invoked inside a view re-runs whenever a signal it read has changed, which makes derived values almost free to declare. Our rule of thumb reserves **`Memo`** for computations that are expensive or that many nodes depend upon, and uses a plain closure everywhere else, because a memo carries its own bookkeeping cost. The simpler option therefore wins by default here.

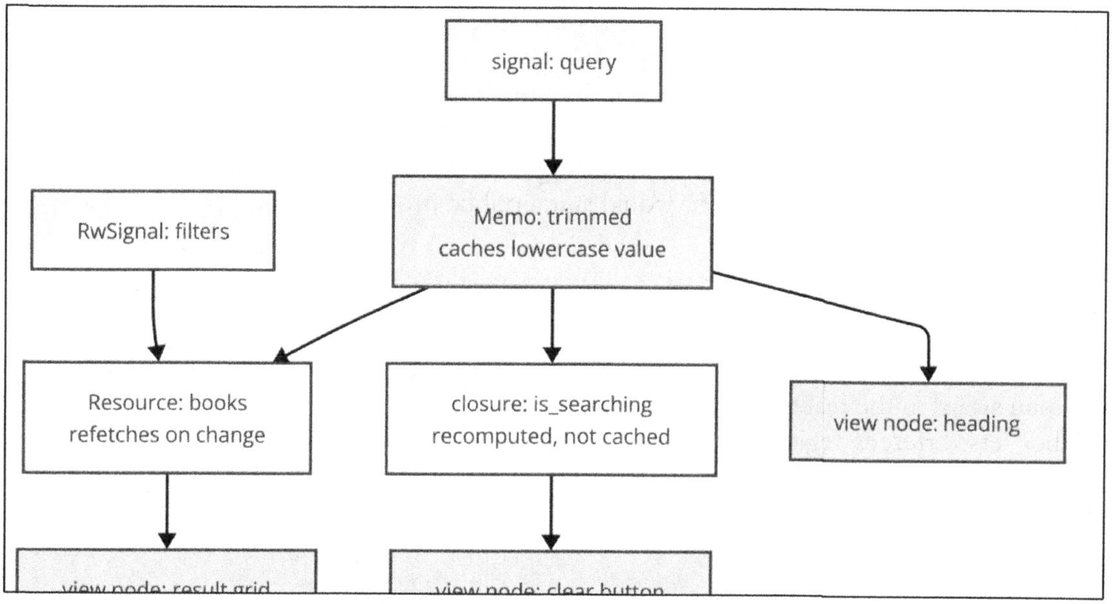

Loading Data with Resources

Our catalogue lives on the server, so the browser must fetch it asynchronously and re-fetch it whenever the search changes. A resource binds a signal to an asynchronous function, re-running that function whenever the signal it watches changes value. The first argument declares what we depend upon, and the second describes how to load the data given that dependency. Both arguments are closures, and the pairing gives us automatic reloading without a single manual subscription anywhere in our code.

```
let books = Resource::new(
    move || (trimmed.get(), filters.get()),
    |(search, filters)| async move {
        list_books(BookFilter { search: Some(search), ..filters
}).await
    },
);
```

Our source closure returns a tuple, which means either input triggers a reload. That arrangement scales neatly as dependencies accumulate, since adding a third filter costs one tuple element rather than a new resource. The source value is compared between runs, and the fetch is skipped entirely when nothing has changed, so a re-render caused by unrelated state never produces a redundant request against our server. A wasted request therefore never reaches our handlers at all, which keeps our server load proportional to real activity.

A pair of variants deserves mention, because they solve problems the plain constructor cannot. The blocking variant delays the server-rendered response until its data arrives, which matters for content that search engines must see in the initial payload. Its local counterpart runs only in the browser and accepts futures that are not Send, which suits work touching browser APIs that have no server equivalent at all. Our catalogue uses the plain constructor throughout this chapter, though the blocking variant would suit a public product listing.

Handling Waiting and Failure with Suspense

A resource begins empty and fills in later, so our view needs a way to describe both conditions. The Suspense component renders a fallback while any resource read inside it remains pending, and then swaps in the real content once every one of them resolves. A boundary nested inside another lets different regions of a view fill independently rather than wait on the slowest request. Our catalogue grid and our recommendation panel can therefore appear independently of one another.

```
view! {
    <Suspense fallback=move || view! { <CatalogueSkeleton/> }>
        <ErrorBoundary fallback=|errors| view! {
            <p class="error">"Could not load the catalogue."</p>
            <ul>{move || errors.get().into_iter()
                .map(|(_, e)| view! { <li>{e.to_string()}</li> })
                .collect_view()}</ul>
        }>
            {move || books.get().map(|result| result.map(|list|
view! {
                <BookGrid books=list/>
            }))}
        </ErrorBoundary>
    </Suspense>
}
```

The two components divide responsibility cleanly between them. Our suspense boundary handles the pending condition, while the error boundary catches any **`Result`** that resolved to a failure, and the pair together cover every outcome a remote call produces. We established earlier that our interfaces return structured problems, so the messages surfacing here carry information a visitor can act upon rather than a generic apology. Both boundaries also compose freely, so either one may wrap the other depending on the granularity we want.

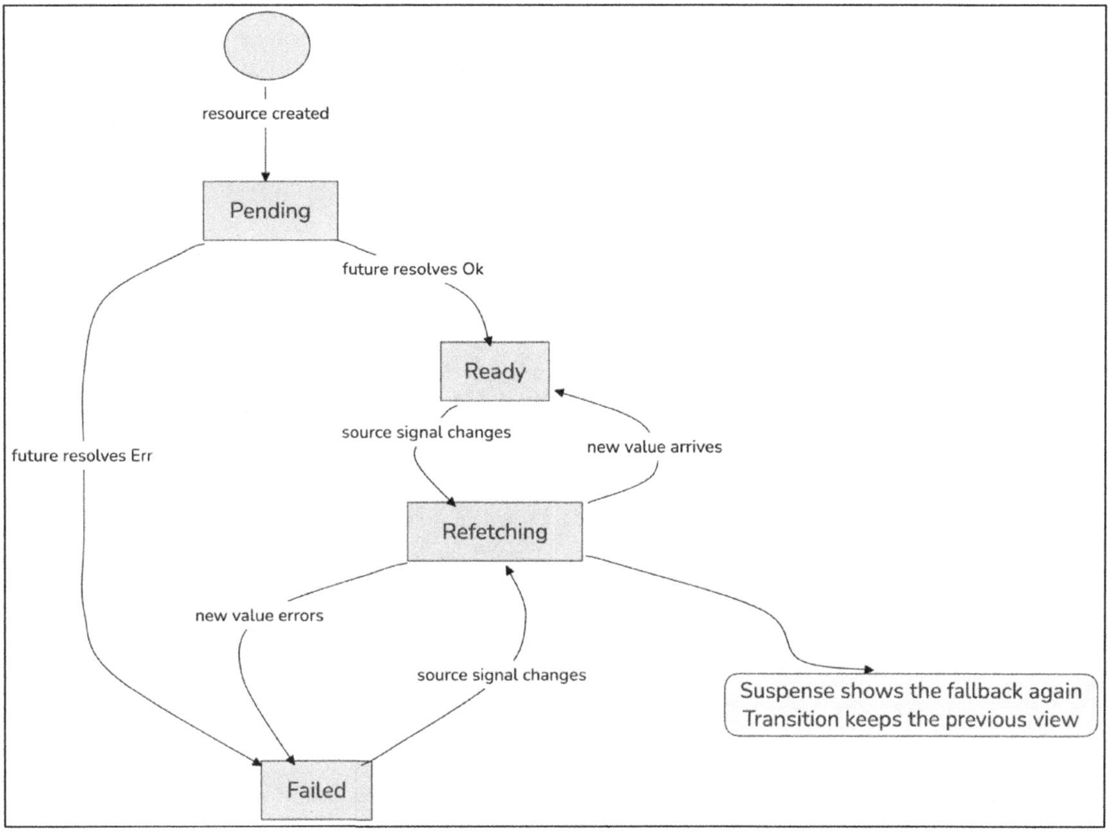

That final distinction matters more than it appears. A **`Suspense`** boundary reverts to its fallback whenever a resource refetches, so a visitor typing into our search field watches the results vanish and reappear with every keystroke. Its Transition counterpart instead keeps the previous content on screen while the new request runs, which produces a far calmer interface for anything a visitor edits continuously. Our search field therefore belongs inside a transition rather than a suspense boundary.

Routing Storefront

Declaring Nested Routes

Our storefront needs several destinations, and the router matches the browser location against a declared tree rather than requiring a request to our server each time. We registered these same routes on the server earlier so the initial render arrives complete, and the client router then takes over for every subsequent navigation. Both halves read from one declaration, which is why they can never disagree. A single declaration therefore serves both rendering paths, and no duplicated route table can ever fall out of step.

```
use leptos_router::components::{ParentRoute, Route, Router,
Routes};

use leptos_router::path;


#[component]

pub fn App() -> impl IntoView {

    view! {

        <Router>

            <NavBar/>

            <main>

                <Routes fallback=|| view! { <NotFound/> }>

                    <Route path=path!("/") view=HomePage/>

                    <Route path=path!("/books/:id")
view=BookDetail/>

                    <ParentRoute path=path!("/account")
view=AccountShell>

                        <Route path=path!("")
view=AccountSummary/>

                        <Route path=path!("orders")
view=OrderHistory/>

                    </ParentRoute>

                </Routes>

            </main>

            <Footer/>

        </Router>

    }

}
```

Whatever sits outside the Routes component persists across navigation, so our navigation bar and footer never re-render when a visitor moves between destinations. That property costs nothing to obtain and removes a whole class of flicker that afflicts naive client routing. Our parent route works the same way at a smaller scale, since the account shell renders once and only the region marked by its outlet changes. A layout that persists is the default here rather than an optimization.

The **`fallback`** argument became mandatory in recent releases, and the requirement is a welcome one. A location matching nothing would otherwise render an empty region with no indication of what went wrong, which is confusing during development and unhelpful in production. Our compiler now insists that we decide what an unmatched location produces before the application will build at all. An oversight of that kind therefore becomes impossible rather than merely unlikely, which is the better guarantee by far.

Reading Route Parameters

Our detail route captures an identifier, and the component behind it needs that value in a reactive form because a visitor may navigate from one book directly to another. A typed parameter struct gives us that value alongside a parse failure we can handle, rather than a bare string requiring validation inside every component that reads it. Our parse happens once at the boundary, and every consumer downstream then receives a value already known to be valid.

```
use leptos_router::hooks::use_params;
use leptos_router::params::Params;

#[derive(Params, PartialEq, Clone, Debug)]
struct BookRouteParams {
    id: Option<Uuid>,
}

#[component]
pub fn BookDetail() -> impl IntoView {
    let params = use_params::<BookRouteParams>();

    let book = Resource::new(
        move || params.get().ok().and_then(|p| p.id),
        |maybe_id| async move {
            match maybe_id {
                Some(id) => find_book(id).await,
```

```
            None => Err(ServerFnError::new("missing
identifier")),
        }
    },
);

view! {
    <Suspense fallback=move || view! { <DetailSkeleton/> }>
        {move || book.get().map(|r| r.map(|b| view! {
<BookPanel book=b/> }))}
    </Suspense>
}
}
```

Our parameter feeds the resource source directly, which produces exactly the behaviour a visitor expects. A move to a different identifier changes the source value, the resource refetches, and the suspense boundary covers the gap without us writing a single line of coordination. The state of a component and the location therefore stay synchronized by construction rather than by an effect we remembered to add. A failure to coordinate the two is therefore not a mistake we are able to make in the first place.

Our choice to wrap the identifier in an **`Option`** also acknowledges something worth stating plainly. A route parameter arrives from a URL that anybody may edit, so a malformed identifier is an entirely ordinary condition rather than an exceptional one. Our parse failure produces a handled error inside the boundary above, and no panic ever reaches the browser console.

Navigating without Reloading

A link inside our application uses a component rather than a plain anchor, which lets the router intercept the click and swap the view without a round trip. The rendered markup remains a real anchor element, so a visitor may still open the destination in a new tab and a crawler still follows it normally. Our accessibility and our search indexing both survive intact, whereas a click handler attached to a plain element would quietly destroy both of them.

```
use leptos_router::components::A;
use leptos_router::hooks::use_navigate;

view! {
```

```
    <A href=format!("/books/{}", book.id) attr:class="card-link">
        {book.title.clone()}
    </A>
}
```

Navigation driven by code follows a different route, since some transitions happen after work completes rather than after a click. Our checkout flow moves the visitor to an order confirmation once the server accepts the order, and the navigate hook performs exactly that.

```
let navigate = use_navigate();
let on_success = move |order_id: Uuid| {
    navigate(&format!("/account/orders/{order_id}"),
Default::default());
};
```

Both mechanisms update the browser history properly, so the back button behaves as a visitor expects throughout. That detail separates a competent single-page application from a frustrating one, and Leptos handles it for us provided we avoid manipulating the location directly. Code reaching for the raw browser location bypasses the router entirely and produces a view that no longer matches the address bar.

Building Reusable Components

Typed Props and Optional Values

Our interface repeats certain shapes constantly, and a component captures each shape once. Each prop arrives as a typed function argument, and several attributes control how callers supply them, which keeps our call sites concise without sacrificing the compiler's checking.

```
#[component]
pub fn BookCard(
    #[prop(into)] title: String,
    #[prop(into)] author: String,
    #[prop(optional)] cover_url: Option<String>,
    #[prop(default = true)] show_price: bool,
    price_cents: i64,
) -> impl IntoView {
```

```
    view! {
        <article class="book-card">
            {cover_url.map(|url| view! { <img src=url alt=""/>
})}
            <h3>{title}</h3>
            <p class="author">{author}</p>
            <Show when=move || show_price>
                <p class="price">{format_money(price_cents)}</p>
            </Show>
        </article>
    }
}
```

The signature carries three attributes, and each removes friction at the call site. An into attribute accepts anything convertible, so a caller passes a string slice where our signature demands an owned string. The **`optional`** attribute lets a caller omit the prop entirely rather than writing an explicit **`None`**. A **`default`** value covers props that usually take one setting and occasionally take another. Our call sites therefore stay short while the compiler continues checking every single argument we pass.

Our **`Show`** component deserves a brief remark, because a plain conditional would also work. An **`if`** expression evaluates once and produces static markup, whereas **`Show`** re-evaluates its condition reactively and swaps its content whenever that condition changes. A fixed condition therefore belongs in an if expression, and anything depending on a signal belongs inside Show. Any confusion between the two produces an interface that renders correctly on first paint and then stops responding to anything at all.

Composing with Children

A component that wraps arbitrary content accepts children, which turns it into a layout rather than a fixed shape. Our panel below supplies a heading and a border while remaining entirely uninterested in what a caller places inside it.

```
#[component]
pub fn Panel(
    #[prop(into)] heading: String,
    children: Children,
) -> impl IntoView {
```

```
    view! {
        <section class="panel">
            <h2>{heading}</h2>
            <div class="panel-body">{children()}</div>
        </section>
    }
}

view! {
    <Panel heading="Recently viewed">
        <BookGrid books=recent/>
    </Panel>
}
```

The children argument is a callable rather than a value, and calling it exactly once is the normal pattern. A component needing to render its children repeatedly takes ChildrenFn instead, which permits multiple invocations at the cost of requiring the closure to be cloneable. Our compiler enforces that distinction, so a component cannot accidentally render children twice when its type promised otherwise. These layout components therefore state their intent through their signatures rather than through a comment nobody reads.

This kind of composition carries a practical benefit for the maintenance question we address shortly. A layout component holding no business logic contains almost nothing framework-specific beyond its markup, whereas a component tangled with data fetching and state management would be considerably harder to port. Anything purely presentational ports to another framework far more easily than a stateful one does, which becomes distinctly relevant later in this chapter.

Submitting Forms with Actions

Our order placement needs a form, and Leptos offers a mechanism combining the reliability of a plain HTML submission with the responsiveness of a client-side one. A server action wraps a server function with pending and result state, and the accompanying form component submits through JavaScript when available and through an ordinary form post when it is not. Both paths reach the identical server function, so our behaviour never diverges between them regardless of what the browser supports.

```
use leptos::prelude::*;
use leptos::server_fn::ServerFnError;
```

```
#[server(PlaceOrder, "/api")]

pub async fn place_order(book_id: Uuid, quantity: i32) ->
Result<Uuid, ServerFnError> {

    let state = expect_context::<AppState>();

    let claims = current_claims()?;

    state.orders

        .place_order(claims.sub, vec![OrderLine::single(book_id,
quantity)])

        .await

        .map(|order| order.id)

        .map_err(|e| ServerFnError::new(e.to_string()))

}


#[component]

pub fn AddToCart(book_id: Uuid) -> impl IntoView {

    let action = ServerAction::<PlaceOrder>::new();


    view! {

        <ActionForm action=action>

            <input type="hidden" name="book_id"
value=book_id.to_string()/>

            <input type="number" name="quantity" value="1"
min="1"/>

            <button type="submit" disabled=move ||
action.pending().get()>

                {move || if action.pending().get() { "Placing…" }
else { "Add to cart" }}

            </button>

        </ActionForm>

    }

}
```

The property worth appreciating here is progressive enhancement. Our form carries a real action attribute pointing at the generated endpoint, so a browser with a failed WebAssembly load still submits it and still places the order. We demonstrated that distinction at the very start with a button that stopped responding, and this form instead degrades to the behaviour the web had before any of this existed.

The pending signal drives our disabled state and our label, which prevents the double submission that impatient visitors otherwise produce. We made our order placement safe against concurrent stock changes at the database level earlier, and this control removes the more common cause of duplicates before a request is ever sent. A guard at each layer costs little and covers a different failure mode. On its own, neither layer would be sufficient, since each one addresses a different cause of duplication.

Shipping and Sustaining Frontend

Measuring and Reducing Bundle Size

Every visitor downloads our WebAssembly bundle before the interface becomes interactive, so its size directly affects how quickly our storefront responds. A release build applies optimizations that a development build skips entirely, and the difference between them is substantial enough that any measurement of the wrong one misleads badly. Our development bundle carries debugging information and no optimization at all, so a figure drawn from it overstates the real download by a considerable margin every single time.

```
cargo leptos build --release
ls -lh target/site/pkg/
```

The output names the compiled artifact alongside the JavaScript loader that instantiates it.

```
-rw-r--r-- 1 dev dev 412K libro_commerce.wasm
-rw-r--r-- 1 dev dev  22K libro_commerce.js
```

Our workspace manifest can shrink that figure further through a profile applied only to the browser build. An optimization for size trades a little runtime speed for a smaller download, which is almost always the correct trade for a bundle sitting on the critical path.

```
[profile.wasm-release]
inherits = "release"
opt-level = "z"
lto = true
codegen-units = 1
```

```
panic = "abort"
```

An abort on panic removes the unwinding machinery entirely, and the browser reloads our application rather than recovering, which is an acceptable outcome for an interface. With link-time optimization and a single codegen unit, the compiler discards far more unreachable code at the cost of a slower build. We apply these settings in our release pipeline later, where build duration matters less than the bytes we serve.

Choosing Leptos in 2026

Whoever adopts this stack deserves an accurate account of its position, so we address it directly rather than leaving it for a surprise later. The Leptos maintainer published a status update in May 2026 stating that the project is feature-complete and will be lightly maintained going forward, with no significant new development expected and an open invitation for additional maintainers. A 0.9 branch exists as an unhurried effort carrying cleanup rather than features.

What that announcement does not mean matters as much as what it does. Our pinned 0.8.19 works, carries no known defect affecting anything we built, and sits on a codebase the maintainer considers complete rather than unfinished. A framework that has shipped every item on its roadmap differs sharply from one abandoned midway, and plenty of widely used software receives exactly this level of attention without anybody noticing. Being finished and being abandoned are genuinely different conditions.

What it does mean is that we should expect slower responses to issues, few new capabilities, and a smaller pool of contributors than the release history might suggest. A team betting a decade of development on this stack should weigh that carefully. One building an application over the next few years, pinning versions as we have throughout, faces a considerably smaller risk than the announcement might first imply. Our own position sits firmly inside that second group.

Our architecture also limits the exposure in a way worth measuring precisely. The application is made of six crates, and exactly two of them contain any Leptos code at all, namely app and frontend. Those four remaining crates would survive a frontend replacement entirely intact, along with every migration, query, transaction, and interface we published. We justified that separation on principle earlier, and the argument now has a concrete number attached to it. The measure is two crates out of six.

Summary

We built a storefront that loads data reactively rather than imperatively. Our signals, memos, and derived closures form a dependency graph that updates only the nodes a change actually affects, while resources bind asynchronous loads to the signals that drive them and refetch automatically. A suspense boundary covers the waiting condition, an error boundary surfaces the structured failures Chapter 6 defined, and a transition boundary keeps content stable through a continuously edited search. Every update touches only what actually changed.

We then declared a nested route tree shared with the server, read parameters in a form that stays synchronized with the location, and composed reusable components through typed props and children. Our order form submits through a server action that still works when WebAssembly fails to load. We closed by shrinking the shipped bundle and by stating the maintenance position of Leptos plainly, including the measurement that only two of our six crates would need replacing. In Chapter 8, we add live updates over WebSockets.

CHAPTER 8

REAL-TIME INTERACTIONS USING WEBSOCKETS

We will now add live updates to LibroCommerce, so a visitor watching a book sees its stock fall as other people buy copies, and a visitor tracking an order sees its status advance without refreshing anything. Every request handled so far began with a client asking, whereas the material ahead lets our server speak first. That inversion changes what our architecture must provide.

We are going to define an event type inside the domain crate, fan those events out through a broadcast channel, and expose the resulting stream through both backends. Our browser then holds an open connection, survives the drops that mobile networks produce constantly, and renders each update reactively. The closing section covers handshake authentication, slow consumers, and the question of whether sockets were the right choice at all. Each of those matters more than the socket code itself.

Pushing Events from Server

Broadcasting Domain Events

Our events describe things that happened rather than instructions to perform, and that distinction shapes the type we declare. A stock level changed, an order advanced, and any interested party may react however it wishes. Our event type lives in the domain crate alongside the models, since it carries no infrastructure, and both the server and the browser must agree on its shape exactly. A divergence between the two would surface only at runtime, which is the worst moment to discover it.

```
use serde::{Deserialize, Serialize};
use uuid::Uuid;

use crate::models::OrderStatus;

#[derive(Debug, Clone, Serialize, Deserialize, PartialEq)]
#[serde(tag = "event", rename_all = "snake_case")]
pub enum StoreEvent {
    StockChanged { book_id: Uuid, remaining: i32 },
    OrderAdvanced { order_id: Uuid, status: OrderStatus },
    PriceChanged { book_id: Uuid, price_cents: i64 },
}
```

The **`tag`** attribute produces an internally tagged representation, so each serialized event carries a discriminator field naming its variant. Our browser therefore inspects one field to decide how to handle a message, and adding a variant later leaves existing clients able to recognize and skip what they do not understand. We established earlier that additive changes preserve compatibility, and the same principle governs our event stream.

Our fan-out uses a broadcast channel, which delivers every message to every subscriber rather than to whichever one asks first. Each connected socket holds its own receiver, and a publisher writes once regardless of how many are listening. The bus lives in the **persistence** crate beside the services that emit events, which broadens that crate beyond storage alone and would justify renaming it to something like **infrastructure** on a larger project. Our own project stays small enough to leave the name alone.

```
use tokio::sync::broadcast;

use domain::events::StoreEvent;


#[derive(Clone)]

pub struct EventBus {

    sender: broadcast::Sender<StoreEvent>,
}


impl EventBus {

    pub fn new(capacity: usize) -> Self {

        let (sender, _receiver) = broadcast::channel(capacity);

        Self { sender }

    }


    pub fn publish(&self, event: StoreEvent) {

        if self.sender.send(event).is_err() {

            tracing::trace!("no active subscribers for event");

        }

    }


    pub fn subscribe(&self) -> broadcast::Receiver<StoreEvent> {

        self.sender.subscribe()

    }
```

```
}
```

Our publish method ignores its failure deliberately, and the reason surprises people the first time. A broadcast send reports an error only when zero receivers exist, which happens whenever nobody currently has our storefront open. That condition is entirely normal rather than exceptional, so treating it as a failure would fill our logs with noise during quiet periods and teach us nothing at all. The trace level therefore records the condition without attaching any alarm to it.

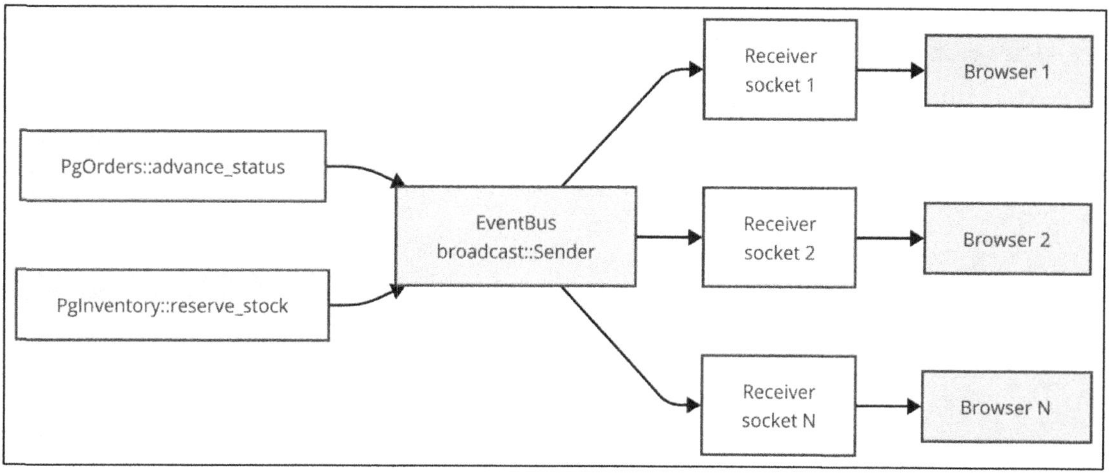

Our persistence methods publish after a transaction commits rather than before it. We established earlier that a rollback discards everything inside the transaction, and an event announced early would survive that rollback and tell every browser about a change that never occurred. That is why we publish on the far side of the commit, where the claim being broadcast is already durable. A mistake of that kind is easy to make and genuinely awkward to notice afterwards.

Upgrading Connection on Axum

A WebSocket begins life as an ordinary HTTP request carrying an upgrade header, and the framework handles that negotiation for us. Our handler receives an upgrade extractor, decides whether to accept, and supplies a closure that takes over the connection once the protocol switch completes. Whatever follows that point runs outside the request cycle entirely. Our handler has already returned by the time the first event travels, and no timeout applying to ordinary requests reaches the connection afterwards.

```
use axum::extract::ws::{Message, WebSocket, WebSocketUpgrade};

use axum::extract::State;

use axum::response::Response;

use tokio::sync::broadcast::error::RecvError;
```

```
pub async fn ws_handler(ws: WebSocketUpgrade, State(state):
State<AppState>) -> Response {
    ws.on_upgrade(move |socket| pump_events(socket, state))
}

async fn pump_events(mut socket: WebSocket, state: AppState) {
    let mut events = state.events.subscribe();

    loop {
        tokio::select! {
            incoming = socket.recv() => match incoming {
                None | Some(Err(_)) | Some(Ok(Message::Close(_)))
=> break,
                Some(Ok(_)) => {}
            },
            event = events.recv() => match event {
                Ok(event) => {
                    let payload = match
serde_json::to_string(&event) {
                        Ok(payload) => payload,
                        Err(_) => continue,
                    };
                    if
socket.send(Message::Text(payload.into())).await.is_err() {
                        break;
                    }
                }
                Err(RecvError::Lagged(missed)) => {
                    tracing::warn!(missed, "subscriber fell
behind");
```

```
                let _ =
socket.send(Message::Text("{\"event\":\"resync\"}".into())).await
;
            }
            Err(RecvError::Closed) => break,
        },
    }
  }
}
```

Our **select!** macro waits on both directions at once and proceeds with whichever completes first. A read from the socket matters even though we ignore the content, because a client closing its connection surfaces as a receive result, and we would otherwise never learn the connection had gone. Any send failure also ends the loop, since a socket refusing writes has already disconnected in some manner we cannot recover from.

A single detail changed between Axum releases, and it catches every upgrade. Previously a string frame accepted an owned String, whereas Axum 0.8 expects a Utf8Bytes value instead, which is why our payload passes through a conversion. The change reduces copying on the hot path, and the compiler reports it clearly enough, though anybody transplanting older example code will meet it immediately. Our conversion costs one method call and removes an allocation that the older signature required.

Serving Same Stream from Actix

Our second backend reaches the same outcome through a rather different shape. The **actix-ws** crate returns three values at once, namely the response we must return immediately, a session handle for writing, and a stream of incoming frames. Our connection loop then runs as a spawned task rather than as the continuation of our handler. That difference is structural rather than cosmetic, since the response must reach the client before any event can travel across the connection we just accepted.

```
use actix_web::{web, HttpRequest, HttpResponse};
use actix_ws::Message;
use futures_util::StreamExt;

pub async fn ws_handler(
    req: HttpRequest,
    body: web::Payload,
```

```
    state: web::Data<AppState>,
) -> Result<HttpResponse, actix_web::Error> {
    let (response, mut session, mut frames) =
actix_ws::handle(&req, body)?;
    let mut events = state.events.subscribe();

    actix_web::rt::spawn(async move {
        loop {
            tokio::select! {
                frame = frames.next() => match frame {
                    None | Some(Err(_)) |
Some(Ok(Message::Close(_))) => break,
                    Some(Ok(Message::Ping(bytes))) => {
                        if session.pong(&bytes).await.is_err() {
break; }
                    }
                    Some(Ok(_)) => {}
                },
                event = events.recv() => match event {
                    Ok(event) => {
                        let payload =
serde_json::to_string(&event).unwrap_or_default();
                        if session.text(payload).await.is_err() {
break; }
                    }
                    Err(_) => break,
                },
            }
        }
        let _ = session.close(None).await;
    });

    Ok(response)
```

```
}
```

The spawned task stays on the worker that accepted the connection, which follows directly from the arbiter model described earlier. Our session handle therefore never crosses a thread boundary, and any state we captured need not be shareable across threads at all. That property becomes valuable once a connection holds something expensive that resists sharing. State held per connection therefore costs us nothing beyond the memory it occupies, with no lock and no atomic operation anywhere.

An explicit reply to a ping is worth the three lines it costs. A browser or an intermediate proxy sends ping frames to confirm a connection remains alive, and a silent endpoint eventually gets disconnected by whichever hop grew impatient. Our Axum handler receives the same courtesy without our involvement, since that framework replies to pings internally, which explains why only one of our two implementations mentions them. Whatever a framework supplies silently is easy to forget once we move to one that does not.

Consuming Stream in Browser

Opening Socket from Component

Our browser side needs the socket API, and we reach it through the generated bindings rather than through an additional wrapper crate. A pair of features covers everything required, and both crates already sit in our dependency graph beneath Leptos.

```
[dependencies]

wasm-bindgen = "0.2"

web-sys = { version = "0.3", features = ["WebSocket",
"MessageEvent", "CloseEvent"] }
```

Our hook opens the connection, parses each arriving message, and exposes the most recent event as a signal that any component may read. An effect runs only in the browser, never during server rendering, which makes this arrangement safe on a page our server renders first. Our server therefore produces complete markup without attempting a connection it could never hold, and the browser then opens its socket only once hydration has finished attaching handlers to that markup.

```
use leptos::prelude::*;

use wasm_bindgen::prelude::*;

use web_sys::{MessageEvent, WebSocket};
```

```
pub fn use_store_events() -> ReadSignal<Option<StoreEvent>> {
    let (latest, set_latest) = signal(None);

    Effect::new(move |_| {
        let socket = match WebSocket::new(&socket_url()) {
            Ok(socket) => socket,
            Err(_) => return,
        };

        let on_message = Closure::<dyn
FnMut(MessageEvent)>::new(move |ev: MessageEvent| {
            if let Some(raw) = ev.data().as_string() {
                if let Ok(event) =
serde_json::from_str::<StoreEvent>(&raw) {
                    set_latest.set(Some(event));
                }
            }
        });

socket.set_onmessage(Some(on_message.as_ref().unchecked_ref()));

        let handle = StoredValue::new((socket, on_message));
        on_cleanup(move || {
            handle.with_value(|(socket, _)| {
                let _ = socket.close();
            });
        });
    });

    latest
}
```

Our closure lives inside a stored value rather than being discarded, and that choice avoids a leak worth understanding. A closure handed to the browser must outlive the call that registered it, and the common shortcut calls **`forget`** to achieve that by leaking the allocation permanently. One stored instead stays alive exactly as long as the component that created it, and the cleanup handler then releases both together.

Our cleanup registration matters equally. A visitor navigating away from the catalogue would otherwise leave the socket open, and repeated navigation would accumulate connections until the browser refused to open more. We established earlier that routing swaps components without reloading, which makes cleanup our responsibility rather than something the browser performs on our behalf. A component acquiring a resource of any kind therefore carries a matching obligation to release it again whenever that component eventually unmounts.

Reconnecting after Drop

In the real world a connection fails constantly, since mobile networks change cells, laptops close, and proxies enforce idle timeouts. A real-time interface therefore needs a reconnection policy, and an immediate retry is the wrong one because a server recovering from an incident would face every disconnected client at once. Exponential backoff with a random component spread that load instead. Our policy therefore protects the server we are trying to reach as much as it serves the client.

```
fn next_delay(attempt: u32) -> Duration {
    let base = 500u64.saturating_mul(1 << attempt.min(6));
    let capped = base.min(30_000);
    let jitter = (js_sys::Math::random() * capped as f64 * 0.3)
as u64;
    Duration::from_millis(capped.saturating_sub(jitter))
}
```

Our delay doubles with each failed attempt, stops growing at thirty seconds, and then subtracts a random portion of itself. Lacking that randomness, every client disconnected by the same incident would return at precisely the same instant, producing a synchronized wave that knocks the recovering server down again. In Chapter 9, we address the server side of that problem, while the client side belongs here. Both halves are needed, since neither one alone prevents a thundering recovery.

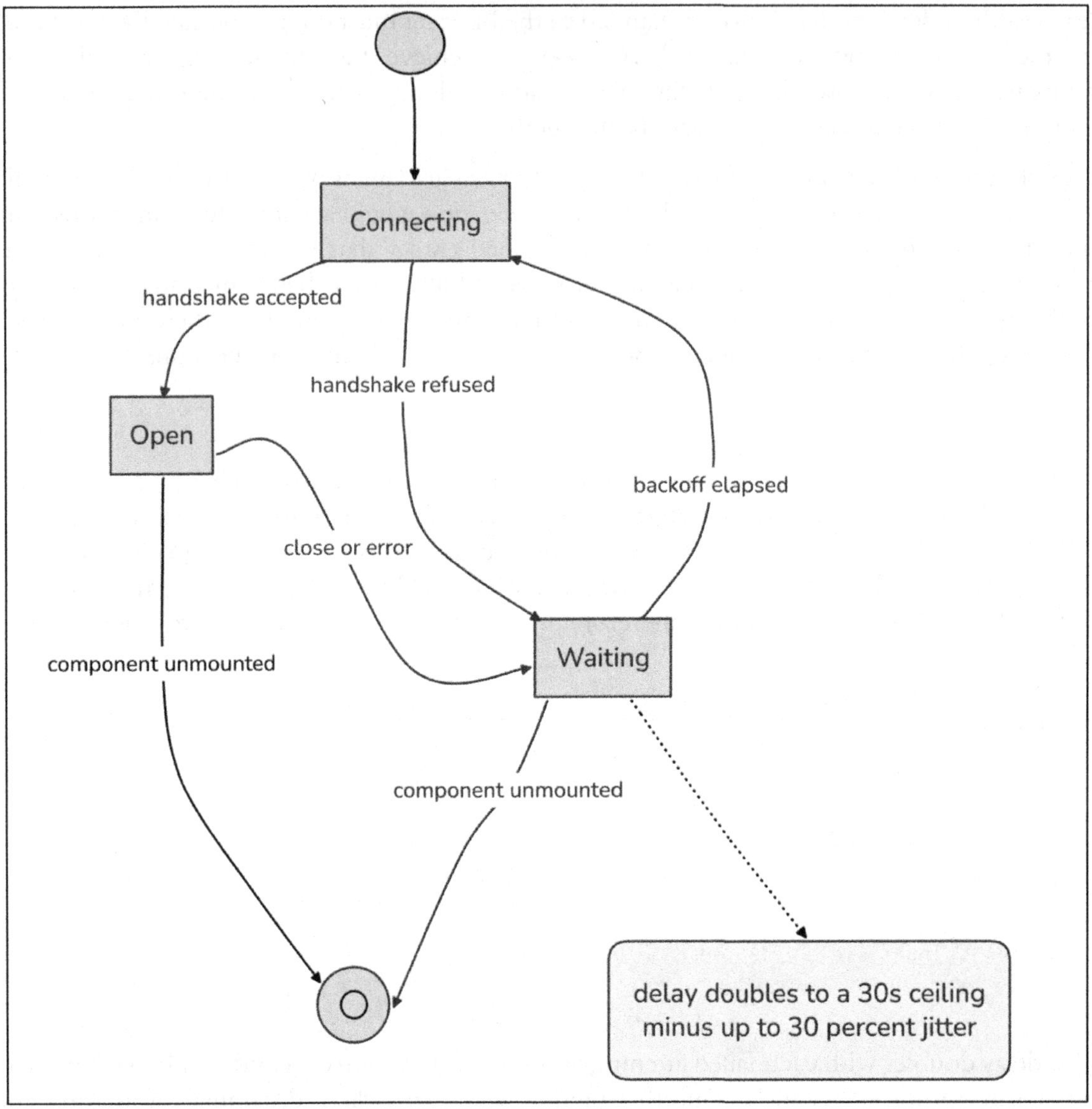

Our attempt counter resets once a connection stays open for a reasonable period, which prevents a slow drift toward the maximum delay. A connection dropping immediately after opening indicates a persistent problem deserving a longer wait, whereas one surviving several minutes before failing suggests a transient network event deserving a prompt retry. Both conditions therefore receive treatment matching what they most likely mean.

Rendering Live Order Status

Our order tracker consumes the signal our hook produces and updates whenever a matching event arrives. We established earlier how resources load initial data, and the socket now supplies subsequent changes, so the component combines both sources rather than choosing between them.

```
#[component]

pub fn OrderTracker(order_id: Uuid) -> impl IntoView {

    let initial = Resource::new(move || order_id, |id| async move
{ find_order(id).await });

    let live = use_store_events();

    let status = RwSignal::new(None::<OrderStatus>);


    Effect::new(move |_| {

        if let Some(StoreEvent::OrderAdvanced { order_id: id,
status: next }) = live.get() {

            if id == order_id {

                status.set(Some(next));

            }

        }

    });


    view! {

        <Transition fallback=move || view! { <p>"Loading
order…"</p> }>

            {move || initial.get().map(|result|
result.map(|order| {

                let current =
status.get().unwrap_or(order.status);

                view! { <OrderTimeline order=order
current=current/> }

            }))}

        </Transition>

    }

}
```

Our effect filters by identifier, because the broadcast delivers every event to every socket regardless of relevance. A filter applied in the browser keeps our server simple at the cost of transmitting messages a given client ignores, which suits an application of our size perfectly well. Any deployment with thousands of simultaneous visitors would instead maintain per-visitor subscriptions on the server, trading complexity for bandwidth. Our choice suits the scale we actually operate at rather than one we imagine.

The initial resource and the live signal cooperate rather than compete. Our resource supplies the status at load time, our signal overrides it once an event arrives, and the fallback expression prefers the live value whenever one exists. A visitor arriving mid-flight therefore sees the correct current state immediately and then watches it advance, with no gap between the two sources. The two mechanisms work alongside one another, one making us right on arrival and the other keeping us right thereafter.

Making Real-time Reliable

Authenticating WebSocket Handshake

Our order stream carries information belonging to particular visitors, so the connection needs authentication, and here the browser imposes an awkward constraint. A socket constructor accepts a URL and nothing else, so the bearer header introduced earlier simply cannot be attached to the handshake. Three approaches exist, and only one of them is genuinely satisfactory. The constraint comes from the browser itself rather than from our chosen framework, so no library can ever remove it on our behalf anywhere.

A token placed in the query string works and is common, though the value then appears in server logs, proxy logs, and browser history, which is precisely where a long-lived credential should never be. Another option is a cookie, since browsers attach cookies to the handshake automatically, and Chapter 9 introduces the session cookies that make this viable. Our preferred approach instead issues a separate short-lived ticket that authorizes exactly one connection and then expires immediately afterwards.

```
pub async fn issue_ws_ticket(
    State(state): State<AppState>,
    Extension(claims): Extension<Claims>,
) -> Result<Json<TicketResponse>, ApiError> {
    let ticket = Uuid::new_v4().to_string();
    state.redis.set_ex(format!("ws:{ticket}"),
claims.sub.to_string(), 30).await?;
    Ok(Json(TicketResponse { ticket }))
}

pub async fn ws_handler(
```

```
    ws: WebSocketUpgrade,
    State(state): State<AppState>,
    Query(params): Query<TicketParams>,
) -> Result<Response, ApiError> {
    let user_id: String = state
        .redis
        .get_del(format!("ws:{}", params.ticket))
        .await?
        .ok_or(DomainError::InvalidCredentials)?;

    let user_id = Uuid::parse_str(&user_id).map_err(|_|
DomainError::InvalidCredentials)?;
    Ok(ws.on_upgrade(move |socket| pump_events(socket, state,
user_id)))
}
```

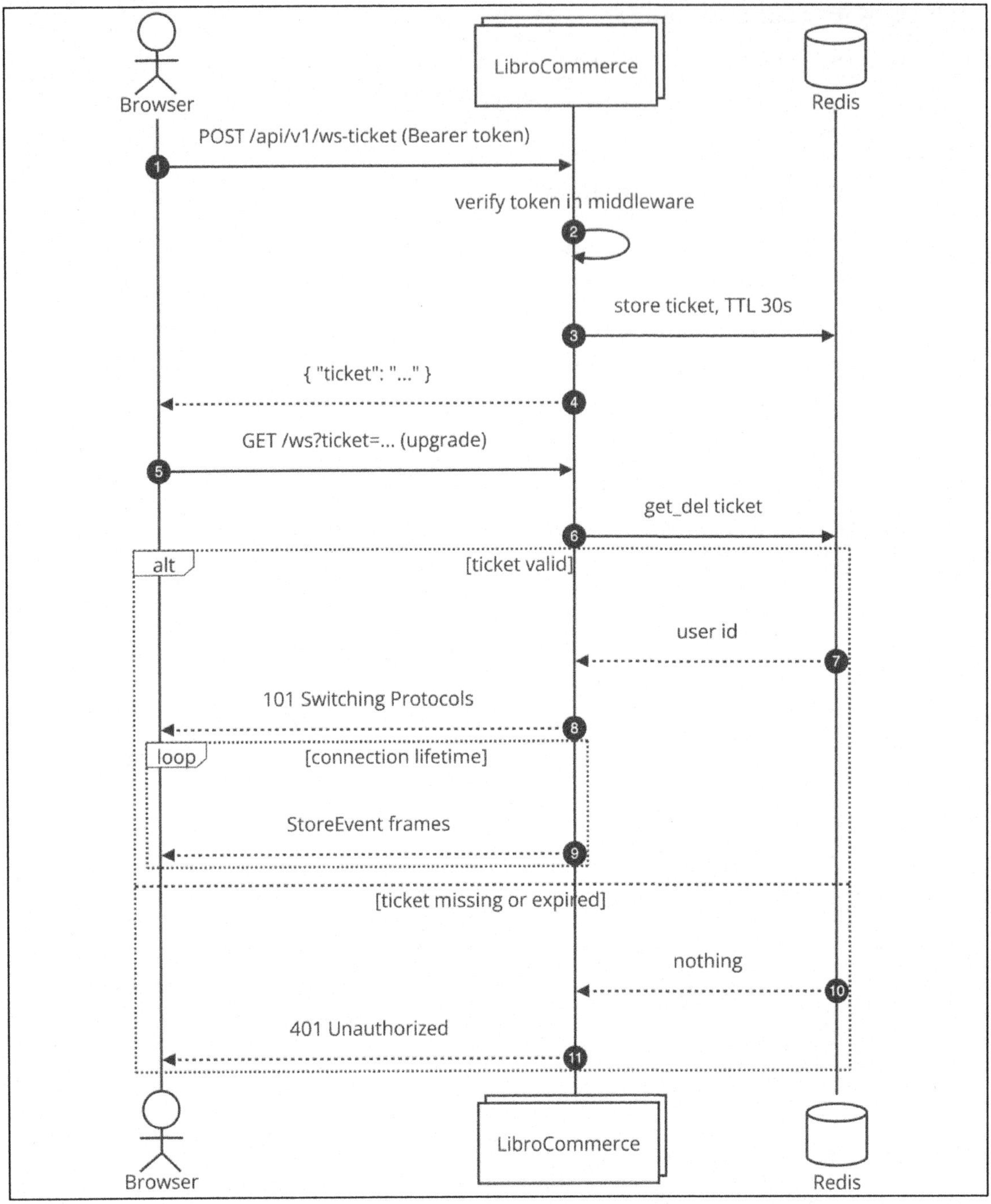

Our ticket survives thirty seconds and exactly one use, so its presence in a log or a history entry costs us nothing once the connection has been established. The retrieval follows the same single-use pattern applied earlier to the authorization callback, and the reasoning transfers directly. A durable credential belongs in a header that never reaches a URL, while a short-lived single-use value may travel wherever convenience demands.

Backpressure and Slow Consumers

A broadcast channel holds a bounded buffer, and a receiver failing to keep pace eventually falls behind the oldest message still retained. Our channel then drops that receiver's missed messages and reports how many vanished, which is where the lag branch in our earlier loop comes into play. That design choice deserves appreciation, since the alternative would let one stalled client consume memory without limit. A bounded buffer protects everybody else from any single misbehaving consumer.

Our response sends a resynchronization instruction rather than attempting to replay what was lost. An attempt to replay would require per-client history, which reintroduces exactly the unbounded storage the channel was designed to avoid. The instruction to refetch the current state costs one round trip and returns it to a correct view immediately, and we already built the resources that perform that refetch.

The capacity of that channel therefore becomes a genuine tuning decision. A small buffer drops messages during brief stalls that a larger one would have absorbed, while an enormous buffer consumes memory proportional to capacity multiplied by message size for every subscriber. Our value of one thousand suits events arriving a few times per second, and Chapter 9 revisits the figure alongside the other limits we set under load. We should settle the value by measurement rather than by intuition.

Choosing between Sockets and Server-Sent Events

We should close by questioning the choice itself, because a real-time feature does not automatically require a socket. A stream of server-sent events travels one way over ordinary HTTP, and our application pushes in exactly one direction, since every message we send travels from server to browser and the client sends nothing but pings. Bidirectional capability that nothing actually uses is simply a cost carried for no return at all, and our storefront sends nothing meaningful upward.

The comparison favours the simpler mechanism on several counts. A server-sent event stream reconnects automatically without the backoff code we wrote, carries cookies without any ticket arrangement, multiplexes over HTTP/2 rather than consuming a dedicated connection, and passes through proxies that mishandle upgrades. The socket wins decisively for two-way traffic, binary payloads, and very high message rates, none of which our storefront actually requires. Our honest assessment therefore favours the simpler mechanism that we did not in fact choose.

Our reason for choosing sockets here is honest rather than technical. The application may later gain features that do send meaningfully from the browser, and a socket accommodates that without a second mechanism alongside the first. An application certain to stay one-directional should prefer server-sent events, and the ability to recognize that distinction matters more than the implementation details either approach demands. Our reasoning is the part that transfers here, rather than the particular selection we happened to make.

Summary

We gave LibroCommerce a live channel from server to browser. Our event type lives in the domain crate as internally tagged data that both sides deserialize identically, and a broadcast channel in the persistence layer fans each event to every open connection. We publish after the transaction commits rather than before, so no browser ever hears about a change that a rollback subsequently erased. The order between the commit and the publication settles that concern entirely.

We then implemented the same stream twice, meeting the **`Utf8Bytes`** change that Axum 0.8 introduced and the spawned-session shape that **`actix-ws`** uses on its per-worker arbiters. Our browser client stores its closure rather than leaking it, cleans up on unmount, and reconnects with jittered exponential backoff. Authentication at the handshake travels through a single-use thirty-second ticket rather than a token in a URL, lagging subscribers receive a resynchronization instruction rather than a replay, and we closed by admitting that server-sent events would have served this application equally well. In Chapter 9, we turn to security, tuning, and monitoring.

Chapter 9

Modern Security, Performance and Tuning

We will now prepare LibroCommerce for conditions that a development machine never produces, namely hostile traffic, encrypted transport, contended resources, and the need to explain a slowdown after it happened. A number of earlier chapters deferred a decision to this one, and each of those debts falls due here, from session storage and login rate limiting through to the connection pool figures we declined to justify earlier. Each of those decisions now rests on a measurement rather than on a preference.

We are going to terminate encrypted connections, send the response headers that constrain a browser, store sessions in Redis behind properly attributed cookies, and size both our runtime and our connection pool against measured behaviour rather than intuition. Our closing sections audit every dependency we ship for published advisories and expose the metrics that explain how a running system is actually behaving.

Securing Transport and Browser

Terminating TLS with rustls 0.23

Our application may terminate encryption itself or receive already-decrypted traffic from a proxy standing in front of it, and both arrangements appear in production regularly. In Chapter 10, we place an ingress controller ahead of our containers, which handles certificates centrally and leaves our binary serving plain HTTP inside the cluster. A deployment running a single instance without that layer needs the capability built in, so we cover it here.

```
[dependencies]
rustls = "0.23"
axum-server = { version = "0.7", features = ["tls-rustls"] }
```

A single line must run before any TLS work begins, and its absence produces the most confusing failure in this entire chapter. The **`rustls`** crate supports several cryptographic backends and declines to choose between them on our behalf, so a process lacking an installed provider compiles perfectly and then panics on its first connection. Not a thing in the type system prevents that omission, which is precisely what makes it so easy to ship without ever noticing it.

```
use axum_server::tls_rustls::RustlsConfig;

#[tokio::main]
async fn main() -> Result<(), Box<dyn std::error::Error>> {
    rustls::crypto::ring::default_provider()
        .install_default()
```

```
        .expect("failed to install the rustls crypto provider");

    let tls = RustlsConfig::from_pem_file("certs/fullchain.pem",
"certs/privkey.pem").await?;
    let app = build_router(AppState::new().await?);

    axum_server::bind_rustls("0.0.0.0:8443".parse()?, tls)
        .serve(app.into_make_service())
        .await?;

    Ok(())
}
```

The resulting panic reports that no process-level provider is available, which describes the cause accurately and still sends most people searching for a certificate problem instead. Our installation call belongs at the very top of the entry point, before any other setup runs, so the failure surfaces immediately rather than after a visitor arrives. Both **`ring`** and **`aws-lc-rs`** work equally well, and our choice of the former keeps the build free of a C toolchain.

Sending Security Headers

A browser enforces a considerable amount on our behalf provided we ask it to, and every instruction travels as a response header. Our application sends the same set on every response, which both frameworks support through a layer applied once at the router level rather than inside individual handlers. We mentioned earlier that Actix bundles a header middleware for exactly this purpose, and every single value below suits either of our two backends without any alteration.

```
use axum::http::{header, HeaderName, HeaderValue};
use tower_http::set_header::SetResponseHeaderLayer;


pub fn security_headers() -> impl Iterator<Item = (HeaderName,
HeaderValue)> {
    [
        (header::STRICT_TRANSPORT_SECURITY,
         "max-age=63072000; includeSubDomains"),
        (header::X_CONTENT_TYPE_OPTIONS, "nosniff"),
```

```
        (header::REFERRER_POLICY, "strict-origin-when-cross-
origin"),
        (HeaderName::from_static("permissions-policy"),
         "camera=(), microphone=(), geolocation=()"),
        (header::CONTENT_SECURITY_POLICY,
         "default-src 'self'; \
          script-src 'self' 'wasm-unsafe-eval'; \
          connect-src 'self' wss://librocommerce.example; \
          img-src 'self' https://covers.openlibrary.org; \
          frame-ancestors 'none'; \
          base-uri 'self'"),
    ]
    .into_iter()
    .map(|(name, value)| (name, HeaderValue::from_static(value)))
}
```

A single directive in that policy is specific to applications like ours, and it catches nearly everybody. An instantiation of a WebAssembly module counts as dynamic code evaluation under the content security policy, so a default policy blocks our entire frontend from starting. The **wasm-unsafe-eval** source permits exactly that operation while continuing to forbid the general **eval** that the older **unsafe-eval** keyword would have allowed.

Our remaining directives close avenues rather than enabling anything. The connect source restricts where our WebAssembly may open connections, which limits what an injected script could exfiltrate, and it must name our socket endpoint explicitly because that scheme differs from the one serving our documents. A frame-ancestors directive set to none prevents our storefront being embedded and clickjacked, replacing the older frame options header with a directive browsers now prefer.

Storing Sessions in Redis

We issued tokens earlier that a client stores and returns, which suits an interface consumed by applications we do not control. Our own browser storefront benefits from a different arrangement, since a session identifier held in a properly attributed cookie cannot be read by injected scripts and disappears the moment we delete the server-side record. Both mechanisms coexist, with tokens serving the published interface and sessions serving our own frontend. The one mechanism does not replace the other, since they protect different kinds of client.

```
pub fn session_cookie(id: &str, max_age: Duration) -> String {
```

```
    format!(
        "sid={id}; Max-Age={}; Path=/; HttpOnly; Secure;
SameSite=Lax",
        max_age.as_secs()
    )
}

pub async fn load_session(redis: &RedisPool, sid: &str) ->
Result<Option<Session>, DomainError> {
    let key = format!("session:{sid}");
    let raw: Option<String> = redis.get(&key).await?;

    match raw {
        Some(raw) => {
            redis.expire(&key, 1800).await?;
            Ok(serde_json::from_str(&raw).ok())
        }
        None => Ok(None),
    }
}
```

The cookie carries four attributes, each defending against a different attack, and omitting any one of them undoes a specific protection. An HttpOnly flag prevents JavaScript from reading the value, so a successful script injection still cannot steal the session. The **`Secure`** flag stops the cookie travelling over plain connections. Our **`SameSite`** setting blocks the cookie on cross-site requests, which defeats forgery attempts originating elsewhere. The maximum age then bounds how long a stolen cookie stays useful.

Our choice of **`Lax`** rather than **`Strict`** for that final attribute deserves justification, since the stricter value sounds preferable. A strict cookie travels on no cross-site request whatsoever, including a top-level navigation, which means the GitHub callback we built earlier would arrive without our session and appear to be an anonymous visitor. The lax setting permits exactly that navigation while still blocking the embedded requests that forgery relies upon. A setting chosen without regard to the flows it interrupts tends to be removed later under pressure.

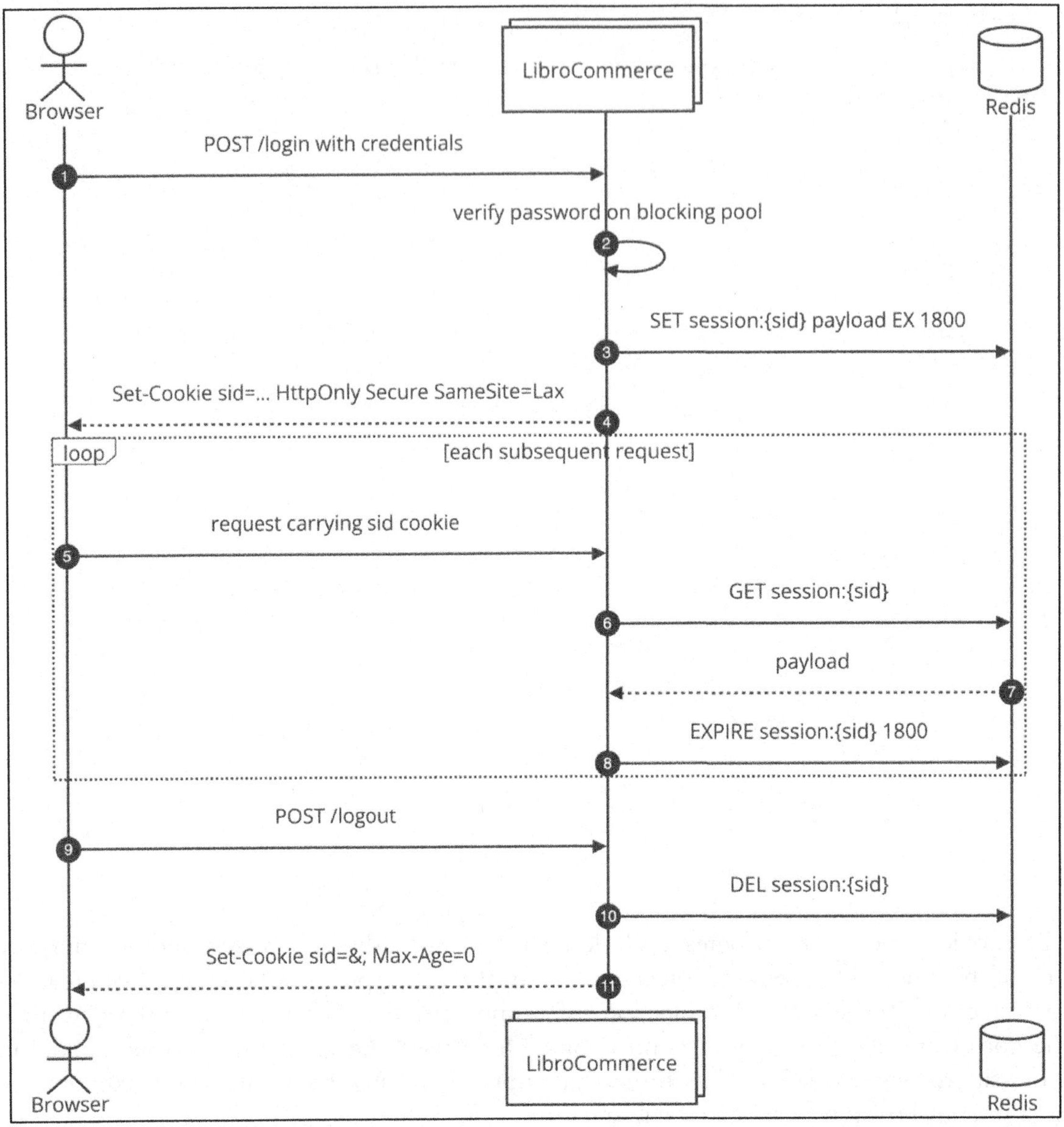

Our expiry refresh on every read produces a sliding window, which is the refresh handling we postponed earlier. A visitor active continuously never gets signed out, while one who walks away loses the session after thirty idle minutes. We can also delete effectively on sign-out here, since a server-side record can be destroyed whereas a signed token remains valid until it expires no matter what we do. The ability to revoke is the property that server-side sessions buy us.

Tuning under Load

Sizing Tokio Runtime

Our runtime spawns one worker per available processor by default, which serves a dedicated machine well and misleads badly inside a container. In Chapter 10, we run our binary with a CPU quota, and the standard parallelism reading reports the host processor quantity rather than the quota we were granted. A binary on a sixty-four core node holding a two-core quota therefore starts sixty-four workers competing for two cores worth of time.

```
fn worker_threads() -> usize {
    std::env::var("TOKIO_WORKER_THREADS")
        .ok()
        .and_then(|v| v.parse().ok())
        .unwrap_or_else(||
std::thread::available_parallelism().map_or(2, |n| n.get()))
}


fn main() -> Result<(), Box<dyn std::error::Error>> {
    tokio::runtime::Builder::new_multi_thread()
        .worker_threads(worker_threads())
        .max_blocking_threads(16)
        .enable_all()
        .build()?
        .block_on(async_main())
}
```

The blocking pool limit matters more here than the worker figure, and our password hashing explains why. Our password verification runs on that pool, Argon2 allocates roughly nineteen megabytes per hash by default, and the pool permits five hundred and twelve threads unless we say otherwise. A batch of five hundred simultaneous verifications would therefore request close to ten gigabytes, and a limit of sixteen bounds that exposure to a few hundred megabytes instead. An exhausted heap under a sudden login surge therefore stops being a plausible outcome at all.

An excess of threads costs us more than memory alone. Every additional worker adds context switching, cache pressure, and scheduler overhead without adding throughput once the processors are saturated. An environment variable lets Chapter 10 supply the correct figure from the very same manifest that declares the quota, so both numbers change together rather than drifting apart over successive deployments. A setting held in exactly one place stays consistent by construction rather than by anybody's vigilance.

Measuring and Sizing Connection Pool

We chose twenty connections earlier and promised a justification, which arrives now through a relationship that removes the guesswork entirely. The concurrent count equals throughput multiplied by duration, so a service handling five hundred requests per second where each holds a connection for ten milliseconds needs five connections on average. Our pool must cover the peak rather than the average, and a factor of three over the calculated figure absorbs ordinary variation comfortably. The earlier figure of twenty therefore sits slightly above what this calculation demands, which is the correct direction to err.

```
requests per second          500
mean connection hold time     10 ms
average concurrency            5
headroom factor                3
pool size per instance        15
instances                      4
total server connections      60
```

The final line is the one that matters most, because our database enforces its own ceiling. PostgreSQL permits one hundred connections by default and spends a full backend process on each, so four instances holding twenty connections apiece consume eighty percent of that allowance before any administrative session connects. Our arrangement therefore stays viable at four instances and breaks at six, which is a limit worth knowing before an incident reveals it. A ceiling discovered during an outage is the most expensive kind.

A deployment exceeding that ceiling needs a connection proxy such as PgBouncer, which multiplexes many client connections onto few server ones. Any large result set deserves separate attention as well, since a query returning fifty thousand rows materializes all of them in memory before our handler sees anything. The fetch method on a sqlx query yields a stream instead, so rows arrive incrementally, and our memory stays bounded regardless of how large the result grows.

Shedding Load

A saturated service that keeps on accepting work degrades for everybody at once, whereas one that refuses the excess early stays responsive for whatever requests it does accept. We established earlier that queueing without a bound eventually consumes everything, and the remedy applies the same reasoning to concurrency rather than to time.

In the following, we bound both of those dimensions together rather than separately, and a request exceeding either one gets refused rather than queued.

```
use std::time::Duration;
use tower::ServiceBuilder;
use tower_http::timeout::TimeoutLayer;

let app = build_router(state).layer(
    ServiceBuilder::new()
        .layer(TimeoutLayer::new(Duration::from_secs(15)))
        .load_shed()
        .concurrency_limit(256),
);
```

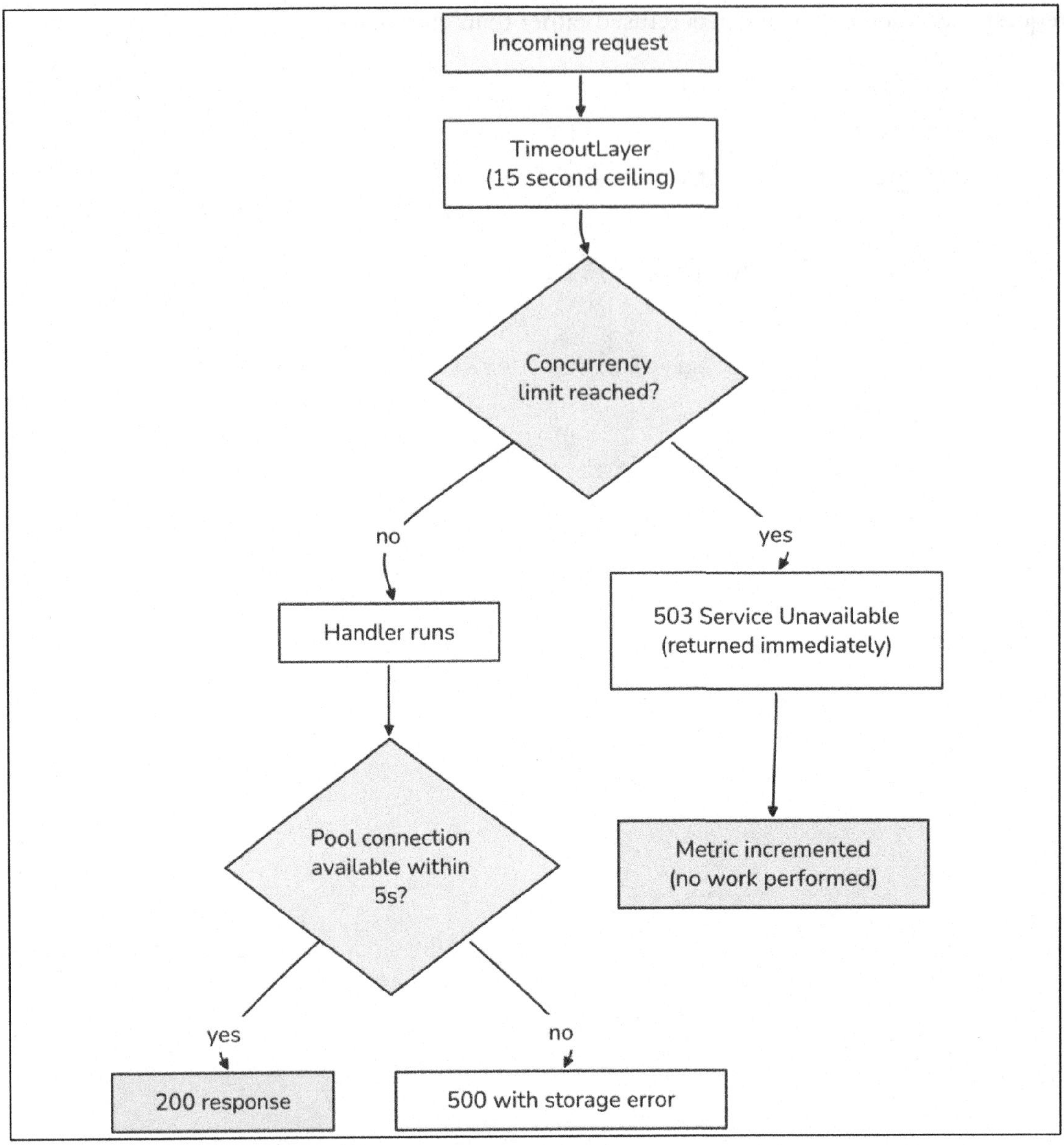

Our ordering places the shed before the limit deliberately, since that combination converts a queue overflow into an immediate rejection rather than a long wait ending in the same outcome. A client receiving a prompt 503 may retry against a healthier instance, whereas one waiting fifteen seconds for a timeout has consumed our capacity throughout. The client-side backoff we built earlier makes such retries safe rather than harmful. Both halves of that arrangement were designed with the other in mind.

Our login endpoint needs a narrower control, which we deferred to this point. A run of password attempts against one account deserves throttling regardless of overall load, and Redis supplies the state without any additional dependency.

```
pub async fn check_login_rate(redis: &RedisPool, email: &str) ->
Result<(), DomainError> {
    let key = format!("login:{email}");
    let attempts: u32 = redis.incr(&key, 1).await?;

    if attempts == 1 {
        redis.expire(&key, 900).await?;
    }
    if attempts > 10 {
        return Err(DomainError::TooManyAttempts);
    }
    Ok(())
}
```

Our key uses the email rather than the network address, which is a deliberate trade carrying a real weakness. An attacker distributing attempts across many accounts from one address escapes this control entirely, so production deployments track both dimensions together. Our version protects individual accounts from focused guessing, which is the more common threat, and we already ensured that a failed attempt reveals nothing about whether the account exists. A pair of defences therefore covers the endpoint together.

Hardening Supply Chain

Auditing Dependencies with 'cargo audit'

Our binary contains code from several hundred crates once transitive dependencies are counted, and any one of them may acquire a published vulnerability after we shipped. The RustSec advisory database records those disclosures, and a tool compares our lockfile against it. We already installed the binaries we need through the same mechanism used for everything else, so nothing further is required.

```
cargo binstall cargo-audit cargo-deny
cargo audit
```

The report names each affected crate alongside the release that resolves the problem.

```
    Fetching advisory database from
`https://github.com/RustSec/advisory-db.git`

      Loaded 782 security advisories

    Scanning Cargo.lock for vulnerabilities (341 crate
dependencies)

    Success No vulnerable packages found
```

The jsonwebtoken decision we made at the outset originated in exactly this process, since the advisory against the ninth release is what forced our move to the tenth. An audit run once during a release is considerably less useful than running it on every build, and Chapter 10 places it in our pipeline so that a newly published advisory fails the next build rather than waiting for somebody to remember. That automation is what turns a practice into a guarantee.

Enforcing Policy with 'cargo deny'

An advisory covers known vulnerabilities alone, and several other supply-chain concerns deserve equal attention from us. A crate appearing at two versions inflates our binary and occasionally produces baffling type errors, an unexpected licence creates legal exposure, and a dependency pulled from an unfamiliar registry deserves scrutiny before it reaches production. One configuration file expresses all of those rules together. Our policy therefore lives beside the code rather than inside somebody's memory, and every rule it holds gets enforced on every single build.

```
[advisories]
yanked = "deny"
ignore = []

[licenses]
allow = ["MIT", "Apache-2.0", "BSD-3-Clause", "ISC", "Unicode-
3.0"]
confidence-threshold = 0.9

[bans]
multiple-versions = "warn"
wildcards = "deny"
deny = [{ name = "openssl-sys", reason = "we use rustls
throughout" }]
```

```
[sources]
unknown-registry = "deny"
allow-registry = ["https://github.com/rust-lang/crates.io-index"]
```

Our banned entry above demonstrates a rule well worth borrowing. Not a single crate in our application should link against the system OpenSSL library, since we chose pure Rust cryptography at the outset specifically to keep our build self-contained, and a transitive dependency quietly reintroducing it would undo that decision without any visible sign. An explicit ban converts that regression into a build failure naming the crate responsible.

The wildcard rule exists to protect the pinning discipline established at the outset. A dependency declared without a version constraint resolves differently over time, which reintroduces exactly the drift our committed lockfile prevents. Both settings cost nothing while everything stays correct and speak up clearly the moment something changes. A rule of that shape is the cheapest kind to maintain, since it demands our attention only at the moment something has genuinely gone wrong.

Observing Running System

Recording Application Metrics

The tracing layer built back at the architecture stage records what happened during individual requests, and metrics cover a different sort of question about aggregate behaviour over time. A set of three measurements covers most of what we need, namely the rate of requests, the proportion failing, and the distribution of durations. Our recording uses a facade so that the storage backend stays replaceable. Those three figures together settle most operational questions we are likely to ask.

```
use metrics::{counter, gauge, histogram};


pub fn record_request(route: &'static str, status: u16, elapsed: Duration) {
    counter!("http_requests_total", "route" => route, "status" => status.to_string())
        .increment(1);
    histogram!("http_request_duration_seconds", "route" => route)
        .record(elapsed.as_secs_f64());
}
```

```
pub fn record_pool(pool: &PgPool) {
    gauge!("db_pool_connections_idle").set(pool.num_idle() as
f64);
    gauge!("db_pool_connections_total").set(pool.size() as f64);
}
```

Our label choices carry a hazard worth stating plainly. Each distinct combination of label values creates a separate series, so a label holding a book identifier or a visitor identifier produces unbounded growth that eventually exhausts the monitoring system rather than ours. A route template and a status code stay bounded by design, which is precisely why we record the matched route pattern rather than the requested path. Discipline about cardinality matters more than any individual metric we choose.

The pool gauges deserve their place because they explain a class of slowdown that request timings alone cannot. An idle figure sitting at zero while durations climb identifies pool exhaustion immediately, which distinguishes a database problem from a slow handler and points at the sizing arithmetic performed earlier. The acquire timeout we established earlier turns exhaustion into a prompt failure, and these gauges reveal the condition before it reaches that threshold. A warning beforehand is worth considerably more than an accurate post-mortem.

Exposing Prometheus Endpoint

The collector gathers figures by scraping rather than by receiving, so our application publishes its current values at a path and Prometheus visits periodically. Our recorder builds the exposition format on demand, which costs nothing between scrapes.

```
use metrics_exporter_prometheus::{PrometheusBuilder,
PrometheusHandle};

pub fn install_metrics() -> PrometheusHandle {
    PrometheusBuilder::new()
        .set_buckets(&[0.005, 0.01, 0.025, 0.05, 0.1, 0.25, 0.5,
1.0, 2.5, 5.0])
        .expect("valid histogram buckets")
        .install_recorder()
        .expect("failed to install the metrics recorder")
}
```

```
pub async fn metrics_handler(State(handle):
State<PrometheusHandle>) -> String {
    handle.render()
}
```

Our bucket boundaries determine which percentiles we can compute afterwards, and the defaults suit slower systems than ours. A Rust service answering most requests in single-digit milliseconds gains nothing from a bucket at ten seconds and loses resolution where its behaviour actually lives. The boundaries above concentrate detail below one hundred milliseconds, which is where a regression in our application would first appear. A bucket chosen for a slower system hides exactly the detail we care about.

Our metrics route belongs well outside the public interface, since those figures reveal internal structure that no visitor has any need to see. In Chapter 10, we bind it to a separate port reachable only from inside the cluster, which keeps the collector satisfied while leaving nothing exposed. A deployment lacking that separation should at minimum place the route behind the authentication middleware built earlier. Our figures deserve exactly the same protection that our data receives.

Summary

We settled the debts that earlier chapters deferred to this one. Our transport now terminates through rustls with the provider installation whose absence produces a first-connection panic, our responses carry a header set including the **`wasm-unsafe-eval`** source that a WebAssembly frontend requires, and our sessions live in Redis behind cookies whose lax same-site attribute keeps the Chapter 6 callback working while still blocking forgery. Every one of those settings was chosen against a specific failure rather than copied from a checklist.

We then replaced guesswork with arithmetic, sizing the worker pool against a container quota rather than a host processor tally, bounding the blocking pool so concurrent Argon2 hashing cannot exhaust memory, and deriving our connection figure from throughput multiplied by hold time against the ceiling PostgreSQL enforces. A shedding layer rejects excess promptly, a Redis counter throttles repeated login attempts, and an audit of our dependencies turns a published advisory into a failed build. Our metrics record rates, failures, and durations under bounded labels. In Chapter 10, we containerize and ship the application.

CHAPTER 10
CLOUD-NATIVE RELEASES AND CONTINUOUS DELIVERY

We will now take everything built across the previous chapters and turn it into something that ships. Our application runs beautifully on a development machine, and the distance between that condition and a reliable production deployment is covered by container images, orchestration manifests, and a pipeline that refuses to release anything failing a check. A number of earlier chapters pointed here, and each of those pointers resolves now. Not a single item in this chapter arrives without a preceding chapter having asked for it.

We are going to build a container image small enough to pull quickly and rebuild fast enough to iterate on, declare the Kubernetes objects that run it, and settle two questions that deployments commonly get wrong, namely which probe should fail when a database goes down and how a terminating instance avoids dropping requests. Our pipeline then gates every release behind formatting, lints, tests, advisories, and query verification. A failure in any one of those prevents an image from existing at all.

Building Minimal Container Image

Writing Multi-stage Dockerfile

Our build needs a full Rust toolchain, while our runtime needs almost nothing, and a multi-stage build lets one file express both. We compile in a stage carrying the toolchain, and only the resulting binary travels into a final stage built from a minimal base. The difference is substantial, since a builder image approaches one and a half gigabytes while our runtime image settles under a hundred megabytes. That time falls in proportion, which matters on every node that schedules our container.

```
FROM rust:1.95-slim AS builder
WORKDIR /app
RUN apt-get update \
    && apt-get install -y --no-install-recommends pkg-config
clang \
    && rm -rf /var/lib/apt/lists/*
RUN cargo install cargo-binstall --locked \
    && cargo binstall -y cargo-leptos@0.3.6

COPY . .
ENV SQLX_OFFLINE=true
RUN cargo leptos build --release
```

```
FROM debian:bookworm-slim AS runtime

RUN apt-get update \
    && apt-get install -y --no-install-recommends ca-certificates
\
    && rm -rf /var/lib/apt/lists/* \
    && useradd --system --uid 10001 libro

COPY --from=builder /app/target/release/server-axum
/usr/local/bin/server-axum

COPY --from=builder /app/target/site /app/site

USER 10001

ENV LEPTOS_SITE_ROOT=/app/site LEPTOS_SITE_ADDR=0.0.0.0:3000

EXPOSE 3000 9090

CMD ["/usr/local/bin/server-axum"]
```

A pair of details in the runtime stage prevents failures that appear only after deployment. The certificate bundle must be present, because our outbound calls to OpenLibrary and GitHub both use encrypted connections and a base image without root certificates rejects every one of them. Our SQLX_OFFLINE setting during the build delivers what we promised earlier, since our compile-time query verification reads the committed metadata rather than reaching for a database that no build container has. Both details cost one line each and prevent a failure that appears only in production.

Our toolchain pin travels automatically, because the rust-toolchain.toml written at the outset sits in the copied source and rustup inside the builder honours it. The base image tag and that file therefore agree by construction rather than by our remembering to update both. A mismatch would surface as a download rather than an error, though a builder fetching a second compiler wastes minutes on every single build. The agreement between the two therefore repays the small attention it demands.

Caching Dependency Layers with 'cargo-chef'

The Dockerfile above rebuilds every dependency whenever any source file changes, because Docker invalidates the build layer the moment the copied context differs. Our dependency graph takes several minutes to compile and changes perhaps weekly, while our own code changes constantly, so separating the two saves an enormous amount of waiting. The **`cargo-chef`** tool exists precisely for that separation. Our build splits into a stage that changes rarely and a stage that changes constantly, which is exactly what Docker layer caching rewards.

```
FROM rust:1.95-slim AS chef
```

```
RUN cargo install cargo-chef --locked
WORKDIR /app

FROM chef AS planner
COPY . .
RUN cargo chef prepare --recipe-path recipe.json

FROM chef AS builder
COPY --from=planner /app/recipe.json recipe.json
RUN cargo chef cook --release --recipe-path recipe.json
COPY . .
ENV SQLX_OFFLINE=true
RUN cargo leptos build --release
```

The planner stage reduces our workspace to a recipe describing dependencies alone, and that recipe changes only when a manifest changes. Our builder then compiles those dependencies from the recipe before any application source arrives, so Docker caches the expensive layer against the recipe rather than against our code. Every subsequent build recompiles only the crates we actually edited.

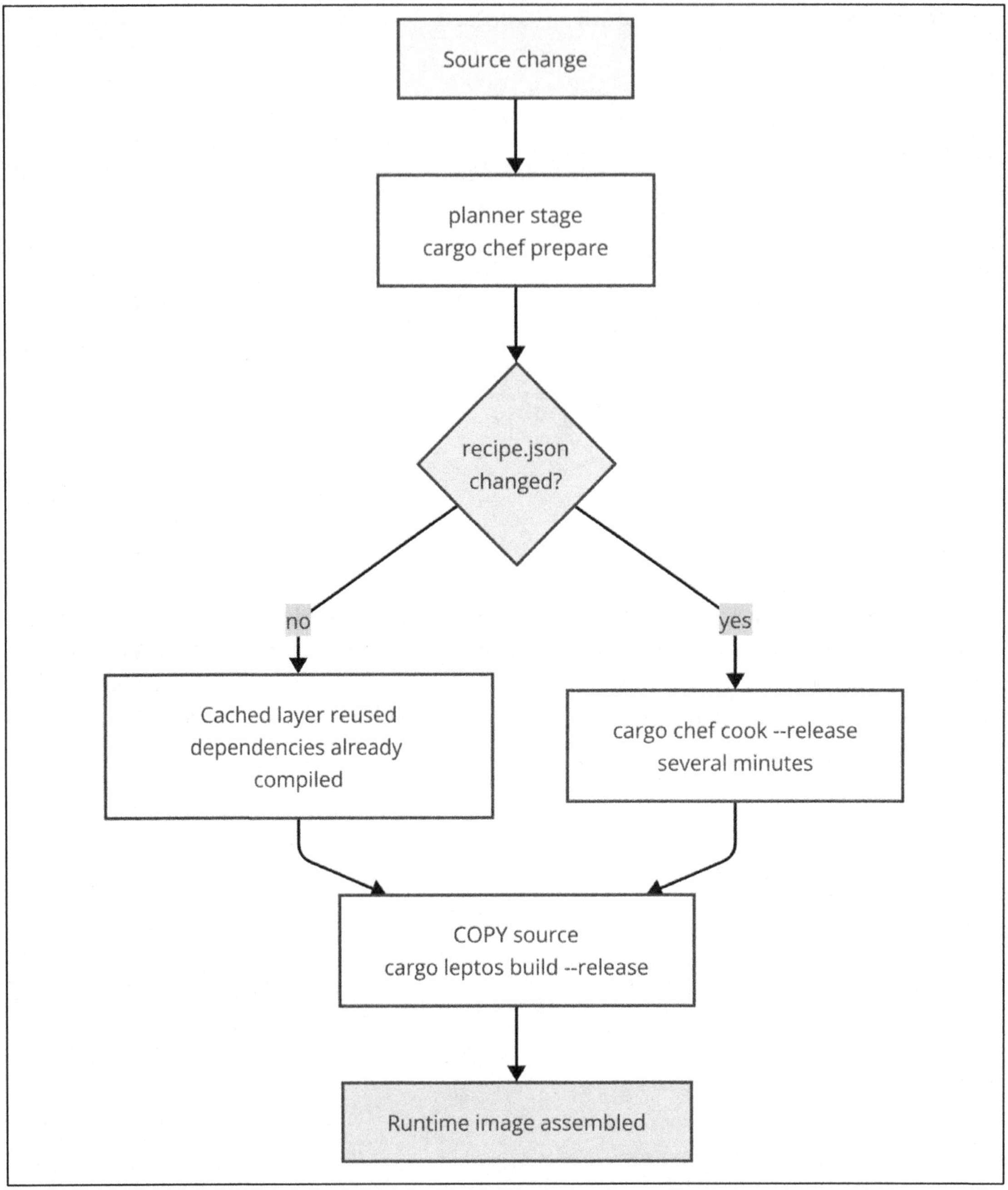

Our measured benefit on LibroCommerce turns a four-minute rebuild into roughly forty seconds whenever only application code changed. We established a size-optimized profile for the browser bundle earlier, and that profile applies here as well, since the release build inside our container uses exactly the settings the workspace declares. The duration of a build matters less in a pipeline than the bytes we eventually serve. Both concerns are nevertheless worth attending to, since a slow pipeline discourages frequent releases.

Running as Non-root User

Our runtime stage creates an unprivileged account and switches to it before the process starts, which limits what a compromised container can attempt. A process running as root inside a container that escapes its isolation arrives as root on the host, whereas an account holding no privileges arrives with correspondingly little. The numeric identifier matters as well, since Kubernetes can enforce a non-root requirement only when it knows the identifier in advance. Our manifest below declares that requirement alongside several related restrictions.

```
securityContext:
  runAsNonRoot: true
  runAsUser: 10001
  allowPrivilegeEscalation: false
  readOnlyRootFilesystem: true
  capabilities:
    drop: ["ALL"]
```

A read-only root filesystem deserves particular mention because our application tolerates it without any adjustment. Our binary writes nothing to disk, since logs travel to standard output and every piece of state lives in PostgreSQL or Redis, so removing write access costs us nothing and closes an avenue an attacker would otherwise use. An application writing temporary files needs a mounted volume instead, which is a reasonable trade for the protection gained.

Deploying to Kubernetes

Declaring Deployment and Service

Our deployment describes how many instances should run, which image they use, and what resources each may consume. The figures below connect directly to the arithmetic performed earlier, since our worker thread setting and our processor limit must agree with one another rather than drifting apart. Both values appear together in the manifest below, which is the only arrangement that reliably keeps the pair honest whenever either one of them changes later on.

```
apiVersion: apps/v1
kind: Deployment
metadata:
  name: librocommerce
```

```yaml
spec:
  replicas: 4
  strategy:
    type: RollingUpdate
    rollingUpdate:
      maxSurge: 1
      maxUnavailable: 0
  template:
    spec:
      terminationGracePeriodSeconds: 45
      containers:
        - name: server
          image: ghcr.io/gitforgits/librocommerce:v1.4.2
          ports:
            - containerPort: 3000
            - containerPort: 9090
              name: metrics
          env:
            - name: TOKIO_WORKER_THREADS
              value: "2"
            - name: DATABASE_URL
              valueFrom:
                secretKeyRef:
                  name: librocommerce-secrets
                  key: database-url
          resources:
            requests:
              cpu: "1"
              memory: 256Mi
            limits:
              cpu: "2"
```

```
            memory: 512Mi
```

A **maxUnavailable** of zero is what makes a rollout invisible to visitors. The cluster starts one additional instance, waits for it to report readiness, and only then removes an old one, so our serving capacity never dips below the declared replica figure. A default configuration would instead retire instances before replacements are ready, which produces a brief capacity reduction that shows up as elevated latency during every single deployment.

Our worker thread variable carries the figure we derived earlier, and the processor limit above it explains why. A container granted two processors would otherwise start one worker per host core, and the two settings living in one manifest keeps them consistent whenever either changes. Our four replicas holding twenty pooled connections apiece also stay inside the PostgreSQL ceiling that the same chapter calculated.

Choosing Probes that Fail Correctly

There are three probes available, and the difference between two of them is the single most consequential decision in this chapter. A readiness probe controls whether an instance receives traffic, while a liveness probe controls whether it gets restarted, and conflating them turns a recoverable incident into a catastrophic one. Our two endpoints below deliberately consult entirely different things, and the difference between the two of them is very much the whole point of this particular subsection.

```
pub async fn livez() -> StatusCode {
    StatusCode::OK
}


pub async fn readyz(State(state): State<AppState>) -> StatusCode
{
    match tokio::time::timeout(Duration::from_secs(2),
state.pool.acquire()).await {
        Ok(Ok(_conn)) => StatusCode::OK,
        _ => StatusCode::SERVICE_UNAVAILABLE,
    }
}
startupProbe:
  httpGet: { path: /livez, port: 3000 }
  periodSeconds: 2
  failureThreshold: 30
```

```
readinessProbe:

  httpGet: { path: /readyz, port: 3000 }

  periodSeconds: 5

  failureThreshold: 2

livenessProbe:

  httpGet: { path: /livez, port: 3000 }

  periodSeconds: 10

  failureThreshold: 6
```

Our liveness endpoint deliberately checks nothing at all beyond the process responding, and the reasoning repays careful attention. A liveness probe consulting the database would fail on every instance simultaneously during a database incident, Kubernetes would restart all four, and the restarts would achieve nothing because the database remains unavailable. Our storefront would then be entirely down rather than merely degraded, and the restart loop would delay recovery once the database returned. We would therefore lose more availability than the underlying fault ever required.

Our readiness endpoint consults the pool because that is exactly the right response to the same incident. An instance unable to reach storage stops receiving traffic and stays running, so a partial failure removes only the affected instances and a full failure leaves everything ready to serve the moment the database recovers. The startup probe covers our initial migration run, granting sixty seconds before the liveness probe begins judging a process that is still preparing. Three probes therefore cover three genuinely different questions.

Shutting Down without Dropping Requests

An instance receiving a termination signal must finish its in-flight work before exiting, and our server needs to be told how. A future that resolves when shutdown should begin is what Axum accepts, and the runtime then stops accepting new connections while allowing existing ones to complete. Our handler work therefore finishes rather than being severed partway through, which matters most of all for any request that has already begun writing something into the database before the signal arrived.

```
use tokio::signal::unix::{signal, SignalKind};


async fn shutdown_signal() {

    let mut term =
signal(SignalKind::terminate()).expect("install SIGTERM
handler");
```

```
    tokio::select! {
        _ = term.recv() => {}
        _ = tokio::signal::ctrl_c() => {}
    }
    tracing::info!("termination signal received, draining
connections");
}

axum::serve(listener, app)
    .with_graceful_shutdown(shutdown_signal())
    .await?;
```

A single subtlety remains, and it produces dropped requests in a considerable number of otherwise careful deployments. The cluster sends the termination signal and removes the instance from service endpoints at the same moment rather than in sequence, and that removal propagates across nodes asynchronously. Our process therefore stops accepting connections while some proxies still believe it should receive them, and a brief pause before shutdown begins closes that window entirely.

```
lifecycle:
  preStop:
    exec:
      command: ["sleep", "5"]
```

A pause of five seconds covers that propagation comfortably in most clusters.

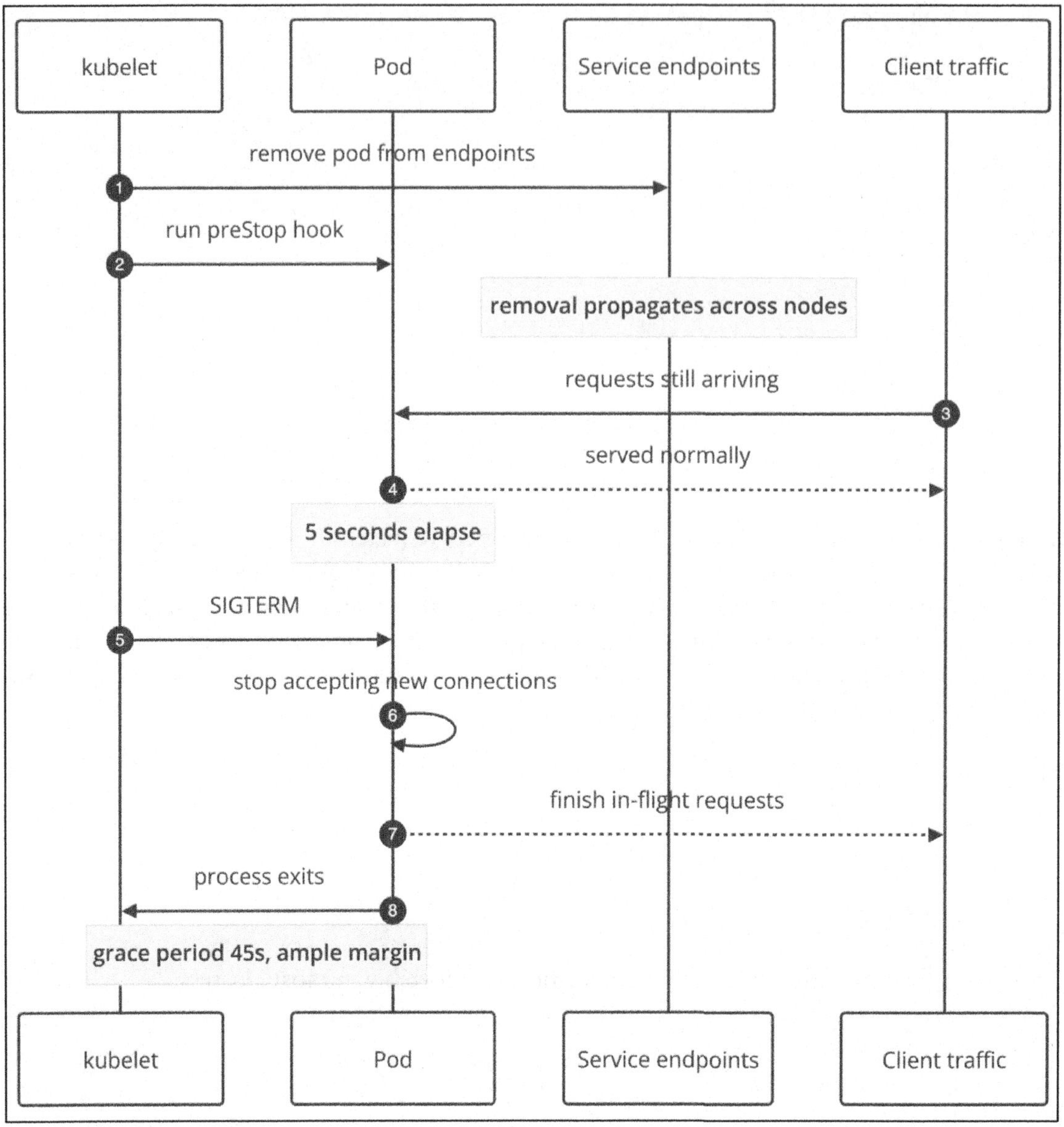

Our grace period of forty-five seconds comfortably exceeds the five-second pause plus any request our timeout layer permits, which we capped at fifteen seconds earlier. The cluster sends a forcible kill once that period expires, so a value shorter than the longest legitimate request would truncate work already underway. A grace period set without reference to request duration truncates work regularly.

Automating Release Pipeline

Triggering on Version Tags

Our pipeline runs on a pushed tag rather than on every commit, which separates the act of releasing from the act of writing code. A commit reaching the main branch still gets checked, whereas only a deliberate tag produces an image and a deployment. That separation means nobody releases by accident, and the tag itself becomes the version everything downstream refers to.

```
name: release

on:

  push:

    tags: ["v*.*.*"]


env:

  REGISTRY: ghcr.io

  IMAGE: ${{ github.repository }}

  SQLX_OFFLINE: "true"
```

Our image tag copies the git tag exactly, which makes every running instance traceable to a specific commit. A moving tag such as latest destroys that property, since two instances pulling at different moments may run different code while reporting the same version. An immutable tag also lets a rollback name precisely what it returns to rather than depend on whatever a mutable label happens to point at. That kind of traceability costs nothing and repays itself during every incident.

Gating Build

Every check that chapter 1, 5, and 9 promised lands in one job, and a failure at any step prevents an image from ever being built. Our gate runs against a real PostgreSQL instance, because the query verification step needs a schema to compare against. We pinned the image tag we reuse here at the very outset, so our pipeline and our development environment now agree on the database version itself as well as on everything else surrounding it.

```
jobs:

  gate:

    runs-on: ubuntu-latest
```

```yaml
    services:
      postgres:
        image: postgres:17
        env:
          POSTGRES_USER: libro
          POSTGRES_PASSWORD: libro_ci
          POSTGRES_DB: libro_commerce
        options: >-
          --health-cmd pg_isready --health-interval 5s --health-
retries 5
        ports: ["5432:5432"]
    env:
      DATABASE_URL:
postgres://libro:libro_ci@localhost:5432/libro_commerce
    steps:
      - uses: actions/checkout@v4
      - uses: Swatinem/rust-cache@v2
      - run: cargo binstall -y sqlx-cli cargo-nextest cargo-audit
cargo-deny
      - run: cargo fmt --all -- --check
      - run: cargo clippy --workspace --all-targets --all-
features -- -D warnings
      - run: sqlx migrate run
      - run: cargo sqlx prepare --workspace --check
      - run: cargo nextest run --workspace
      - run: cargo audit
      - run: cargo deny check
```

The step invoking cargo sqlx prepare with a check flag settles the promise made earlier. Our committed metadata gets regenerated against the migrated schema and compared with what the repository holds, so a query changed without a matching regeneration fails here rather than confusing somebody days later. We asked for the advisory scan on every build earlier, and the two final steps deliver exactly that. Not one of those two promises now depends on anybody remembering to run a command by hand.

Our lint step reproduces the Zed task configured at the outset, which means a contributor running that task locally sees the identical outcome. A gate that differs between a developer machine and a pipeline wastes enormous effort, since failures then appear only after pushing and nobody can reproduce them. One command in both places removes that entire category of frustration.

Deploying and Rolling Back

Our remaining jobs build the image and update the cluster, each depending on the previous one so that nothing proceeds past a failure. The layer cache carries across pipeline runs through the registry, which keeps our image builds nearly as fast as local ones.

```
  image:
    needs: gate
    runs-on: ubuntu-latest
    permissions:
      packages: write
    steps:
      - uses: actions/checkout@v4
      - uses: docker/setup-buildx-action@v3
      - uses: docker/login-action@v3
        with:
          registry: ${{ env.REGISTRY }}
          username: ${{ github.actor }}
          password: ${{ secrets.GITHUB_TOKEN }}
      - uses: docker/build-push-action@v6
        with:
          push: true
          tags: ${{ env.REGISTRY }}/${{ env.IMAGE }}:${{
github.ref_name }}
          cache-from: type=gha
          cache-to: type=gha,mode=max

  deploy:
    needs: image
```

```
    runs-on: ubuntu-latest
    steps:
      - name: Point the deployment at the new image
        run: |
          kubectl set image deployment/librocommerce \
            server=${{ env.REGISTRY }}/${{ env.IMAGE }}:${{ 
github.ref_name }}
          kubectl rollout status deployment/librocommerce --
timeout=5m
```

Our wait on the rollout status turns the pipeline into a genuine verification rather than a hopeful instruction. The cluster reports success only once every replacement instance passes its readiness probe, so a release that fails to start marks the pipeline red instead of appearing to succeed while the previous version quietly stays in place. Our five-minute ceiling then bounds how long a stuck rollout occupies the pipeline. A failure surfaces promptly rather than through a silent divergence between what we released and what actually runs.

A recovery needs one command, and the deployment history makes it possible.

```
kubectl rollout undo deployment/librocommerce
kubectl rollout status deployment/librocommerce --timeout=5m
```

That command returns to the previously running image using the identical zero-unavailable strategy, so a rollback is as invisible to visitors as the deployment that preceded it. A migration complicates the picture and deserves a closing caution, since a rollback returns the code while leaving the schema exactly where the failed release left it. We insisted on reversible migrations for precisely this moment, and additive schema changes deployed ahead of the code that uses them keep the two directions independent.

Summary

With this chapter, we successfully turned a working app into a shipping one. Our container image builds in two stages, caches its dependency compilation through a recipe that changes only when a manifest does, and runs as an unprivileged account on a read-only filesystem carrying nothing beyond a binary, the site assets, and a certificate bundle. The offline flag set during the build resolves our compile-time query verification without any database, exactly as Chapter 5 arranged.

We then declared a deployment whose processor limit and worker thread setting agree by construction, separated readiness from liveness so a database incident degrades our service rather than restarting every instance into a failing loop, and paired a graceful shutdown with a brief pause that covers the endpoint propagation window. Our pipeline triggers on version tags, gates on formatting, lints, query drift, tests, and advisories before any image exists, deploys by waiting on readiness rather than by assuming it, and rolls back through one command against an immutable tag.

Thank You

Index

A

B

C

D

E

F

G

H

I

J

K

L

M

N

O

P

Q

R

S

T

U

W

Z

Epilogue

Well, you now have a working application, which was the whole point. My guess is that the most useful thing you'll get out of it isn't the app itself. If you look back at what actually happened, you'll see what I mean. In Chapter 2, we put the models, the service traits and one error type into a crate that didn't know anything about the web. It felt a bit like a ceremony at the time. There weren't any handlers, no database, nothing running. And then in Chapter 4, we rebuilt the whole server on a different framework, but the domain crate didn't change at all. In Chapter 5, we swapped hash maps for PostgreSQL and neither backend picked up on it. So, in Chapter 6, both frameworks had the same GraphQL schema with handler bodies that were exactly the same, line for line.

None of that was luck. It was the return on a decision made before anything worked.

I also want to mention the cost, because a book that only shows the wins is not being honest. That separation forced us to write conversion code between our enums and the database ones. It stopped us from putting a convenient derive on a domain type. It made us route SQL errors through a helper function rather than a trait implementation. All of those were a real pain, and I had to pay for them over and over again, in exchange for a benefit that only turned up way later in the book. That's how architectural discipline usually feels from the inside. It's a bit annoying at first, but then it suddenly becomes really important.

The clearest illustration came out of the blue. When we talked about Leptos moving into light maintenance, I worked out how much a frontend replacement would cost: two crates out of six. The domain, the persistence layer, and both servers would survive intact, along with every migration, query, transaction, and published interface. That number came about because of a decision made in Chapter 2, and it transforms an anxious question into a regular one.

So here's what I'd like you to take away from this. The best approach is to set your boundaries before you need them, because otherwise you'll have to pay more. Then just pin what you need and commit the lockfile. If you can, go for versions that have been stable rather than ones that are new. So, work out the numbers you need and write them down. Just be honest with yourself about the health of what you're building on, and design it so that being wrong won't be a disaster.

Rust is a language that rewards you for being slightly out of your depth, because the compiler will meet you there and help you to get things right. That conversation is the whole point. LibroCommerce was never the end goal. It was a good place to get my thinking cap on and work on my problem-solving skills without the pressure of real-life consequences. Whatever you build next, the stakes will be higher and the thinking will be the same.

Just try making something that will outlive the dependencies.

Made in the USA
Coppell, TX
05 November 2026

11299184R00111